Safe Is Not Enough

Youth Development *and* Education Series

Series edited by Michael Sadowski

OTHER BOOKS IN THIS SERIES

Make Me!
Eric Toshalis

Schooling for Resilience
Edward Fergus, Pedro Noguera, and Margary Martin

I Can Learn from You
Michael Reichert and Richard Hawley

Portraits of Promise
Michael Sadowski

Safe Is Not Enough

Better Schools for LGBTQ Students

Michael Sadowski

HARVARD EDUCATION PRESS
CAMBRIDGE, MASSACHUSETTS

Paperback ISBN 978-1-61250-942-6
Library Edition ISBN 978-1-61250-943-3

Library of Congress Cataloging-in-Publication Data

Names: Sadowski, Michael, author.
Title: Safe is not enough : better schools for LGBTQ students / Michael
    Sadowski.
Other titles: Youth Development and Education series.
Description: Cambridge, Massachusetts : Harvard Education Press, [2016] |
    Series: Youth Development and Education series | Includes bibliographical
    references and index.
Identifiers: LCCN 2016003319| ISBN 9781612509426 (pbk.) | ISBN 9781612509433
    (library edition)
Subjects: LCSH: Lesbian students—United States. | Gay students—United
    States. | Bisexual students—United States. | Transgender
    youth—Education—United States. | Sexual minorities—Education. |
    Homosexuality and education—United States.
Classification: LCC LC2575 .S23 2016 | DDC 371.826/60973—dc23
LC record available at https://lccn.loc.gov/2016003319

Published by Harvard Education Press,
an imprint of the Harvard Education Publishing Group

Harvard Education Press
8 Story Street
Cambridge, MA 02138

Cover Design: Ciano Design
Cover Images: Jeffrey Coolidge/Getty Images; iStock.com/Fredex8
The typefaces used in this book are Berkeley Oldstyle and Optima LT

CONTENTS

FOREWORD

It's About Time

> *Is safety the only thing to which LGBTQ students are entitled at school? . . . Safety is an essential baseline for schools' ability to meet the needs of LGBTQ students effectively . . . but it is not a sufficient goal in itself [Sadowski's emphasis].*

WHEN I READ THESE WORDS in the manuscript for Michael Sadowski's amazing new book *Safe Is Not Enough: Better Schools for LGBTQ Students*, I practically leapt out of my seat. "*Finally!*" I thought, "Somebody has said it."

For you to understand my alacrity, I need to take you back in time, specifically to 1992.

In 1992 I was a high school history teacher in Concord, Massachusetts, where we had started the nation's first gay-straight alliance in 1988, leading me to found GLSEN (the Gay, Lesbian and Straight Education Network) in 1990. This work had brought me to the attention of our new governor, William Weld, a forward-thinking Republican who was concerned about the high rates of suicide among youth who were lesbian or gay. (We had yet to add "bisexual," "transgender," "questioning," or "queer" to our lexicon.) He created a Governor's Commission on Gay and Lesbian Youth and appointed me to it. I was asked to cochair the education committee, and we made schools our first order of business.

Throughout 1992 we held hearings around the state and heard heartrending tales of the harassment and abuse LGBTQ youth faced at the hands of their peers and (sadly, too often) their families. We learned of the horrible toll exacted by growing up in a society that is fundamentally hostile to your very existence (a toll many of us remembered all too well from our own childhoods). We gathered the then-very-sparse academic data on the experiences of LGBTQ youth and talked to the then-very-few experts on the subject. We set about writing a report with detailed recommendations for what could be done to make schools better places for LGBTQ students.

As we formulated the report and our recommendations, two critical debates that would have long-lasting repercussions for what would become known as the "safe schools" movement dominated our proceedings.

The first was what to call our report. Perhaps befitting her professional background as a therapist, my cochair, Dr. Doris Held, argued for the title "Breaking the Silence." I disagreed. I knew that many folks did not want to break the silence (including soon-to-be-President Clinton, who would promulgate the infamous "don't ask, don't tell" policy for LGBTQ members of the military the next year). I felt that such a frame would appeal only to those who already agreed with us that such a silence was unhealthy (which, for the record, it is—Doris was right about that) and that we needed a more universal theme around which people of all different viewpoints could rally. I argued that theme should be "safe schools": everyone could agree that kids had a right to be safe at school and, furthermore, the many tales about the consequences of the lack of safety in our schools made the need for action abundantly apparent. Our chair, David LaFontaine, and the bulk of the commissioners agreed with me while also seeing the logic and wisdom of Dr. Held's argument, so we settled on a compromise: *Making Schools Safe for Gay and Lesbian Youth: Breaking the Silence in Schools and in Families.*

The next debate was what to include in the report. Certain recommendations we made—like the need for a statewide law protecting LGBTQ youth from discrimination—were quickly affirmed. But we got stuck on the issue of curriculum. Working with a task force of educators, I had formulated detailed recommendations for curricular inclusion across all subject matters and ages. The overwhelming majority of the commission rejected these, saying they were simply politically impossible to advance in the wake of the controversy in New York City about its "Children of the Rainbow" curriculum (which had resulted in the chancellor losing his job). We ended up settling on a rather mild plea for curricular inclusion (with no specifics as to what that meant), and sent the report to the governor in February 1993.

To Weld's credit, he immediately welcomed the report and vowed to implement its recommendations, save one: curriculum. He distanced himself from this aspect of the report (so much so that the headline on the front page of the next day's *Boston Herald* read "Weld: There Will Be No Gay School Lessons"), and it basically got dropped as the state went on to formulate its first-in-the-nation "Safe Schools for Gay and Lesbian Students" program.

For more than two decades this has nagged at me. While my fellow commissioners were probably right that there were very real limits as to what we could expect schools to do in the early nineties (when same-sex sexual relations were still illegal in many states, mind you) and did the politically smart thing in overruling me, I have always regretted that we settled for less than what we knew was required. As Michael writes in his introduction, "Is safety the only thing to which LGBTQ students are entitled at school?" In 1993, I guess it was, but that never sat well with me.

If anyone is to blame for the dominance of the safe schools frame—with all its limitations—for the next two decades, it has to be me. I took the Massachusetts model nationwide when GLSEN became a national organization in 1994 and for nearly two decades beat the "safety" drum hard, first as executive director of GLSEN until 2008 and then as President Obama's Assistant Deputy Secretary for Safe and Drug-Free Schools from 2009 to 2011. The conflagrations that even this seemingly mild and noncontroversial frame inspired (including an effort by over sixty House Republicans to have me removed from office in December 2009) showed that it was and remains politically volatile to ask schools to address LGBTQ concerns. But the safety argument always involved a bit of tongue biting on my part. I knew that for LGBTQ students to truly thrive, not just survive, safety, as Michael writes, "*is not a sufficient goal in itself.*" It just never felt politically possible to say it.

Well, now someone has, and thank God for that.

Michael Sadowski's book is a much-needed and long-overdue "upgrade" of the safe schools movement, moving us beyond what is politically possible to what is educationally required for LGBTQ students to thrive. Michael makes a compelling case, with specific and highly practical examples, for schools to go beyond mere safety to full inclusion for LGBTQ students. His analysis is sophisticated, taking into account not only sexual orientation and gender identity but also factors such as students' age, race, class, religion, and region (to name a few). Michael offers every reader—regardless of whom they teach, or where they teach—useful takeaways for creating meaningful change in their schools. In short, he has given us a roadmap for the next phase of this movement.

I for one will forever be in his debt for correcting the well-intentioned mistakes we made two decades ago. This is the most important book written on LGBTQ issues in education in my lifetime, and I am honored to introduce it to you. Enjoy!

Kevin Jennings
Executive Director
Arcus Foundation

INTRODUCTION

Beyond "Safe" Schools

Educating the Next Generation of LGBTQ Students

An education that creates silence is not an education.

—Roger Simon[1]

F OR CENTURIES American educators, philosophers, educational historians, researchers, and policy makers have grappled with and debated the most fundamental question of all about public schooling in the United States: *What is it for?* To what ideal should it aspire? Do children attend school so that they can become active, engaged participants in our democracy? To develop the knowledge and skills needed to assume a satisfying vocation? To learn how to use their minds well and grapple with complex intellectual questions?

At a practical level, these ideals are not mutually exclusive—few educators aspire to one and only one—and certainly many other theories and philosophies about the primary reasons we send children to school exist in addition to those discussed here. It is beyond the scope of this book to address this far-reaching question, regardless of how engaging or important it might be. Yet a common thread connecting all these goals is a focus on *optimal learning and development*—nurturing the knowledge and skills of children and adolescents so that they might achieve to their full potential, whatever one might think that highest level of achievement should look like or to what end it should lead.

Few educators or philosophers of education would argue that schools' sole purpose is to keep children safe. Yet a particular subset of students in the United States—lesbian, gay, bisexual, transgender, queer, and questioning (LGBTQ)* students—are often served by their schools as if their mere safety were a sufficient objective in and of itself.[2] This book's purpose is to challenge the all-too-prevalent attitudes and practices that suggest "safe" schools are enough for LGBTQ students, and to articulate what it might look like to take public schools in the United States to the next level in their service to LGBTQ students and their treatment of LGBTQ issues. Fortunately, this vision need not emerge out of some utopian vision of the future. Today, right now, educators working in different parts of the country and in various capacities—as teachers, administrators, librarians, and counselors—realize aspects of this vision every day with their students. Their efforts illustrate not only that schools *should be* more than safe for LGBTQ students but that they *already are* in many respects, in a wide range of communities and contexts around the country, and that they therefore *can be* in many others.

"SAFE" SCHOOLS AND HOW WE GOT THERE

Safety is, of course, a basic prerequisite for schooling—children and adolescents need to feel and be safe at school in order to learn. The language of safety has therefore been central to programming in support of LGBTQ students throughout its often-contentious history over the last three decades.

---

* In discussions of the issues that affect LGBTQ students, language can be problematic. Before the 1990s, most studies about LGBTQ people referred only to lesbian (L) and gay (G) individuals, but researchers have become increasingly aware that bisexual (B) people are a distinct group with specific concerns. More recent research also has recognized the special issues that affect transgender (T) individuals, those who do not conform to traditional man/woman or boy/girl gender norms in a variety of ways. (See chapter 5 for a more detailed discussion of transgender identity.) In addition, some individuals identify as queer (Q), a designation that implies a rejection of societal norms and/or labels associated with sexuality and gender. The Q in LGBTQ is also used to designate "questioning" here, referring to students who are unsure of their sexual orientation or gender identity. When citing sources that use different abbreviations such as "LGBT," I use those abbreviations in the interest of accuracy.

The universal belief in the need for students to be safe at school was key to the arguments educators and activists made in the 1980s and early 1990s, when efforts to improve schools for LGBTQ (or, as was the focus at the time, gay and lesbian) youth were in their early stages. As these education advocates urgently and accurately pointed out, gay and lesbian students were being verbally and physically harassed on a daily basis at school, did not feel safe, and were suffering a host of academic, health, and mental health consequences because of it—conditions that persist in many school environments to this day.

In 1989, Massachusetts was the first state to tackle the issues affecting LGBTQ youth in schools and communities by establishing what was then called the Governor's Commission on Gay and Lesbian Youth.[3] Although it was a tough sell in that era, even in relatively progressive Massachusetts, advocates succeeded at getting Republican governor William Weld to issue an executive order starting the Commission primarily by highlighting the public health epidemic of gay and lesbian youth suicide. National statistics at the time showed that about a third of adolescent suicides were by gay and lesbian young people, a crisis advocates argued could be addressed through community- and school-based programs that made these environments safer for gay and lesbian students.[4]

Eventually, the commission's work led to the nation's first state-funded programs to benefit gay and lesbian youth, and policy makers made the language of safety prominent in these initial efforts. Massachusetts' school-based program, first founded in 1993, was and continues to be called the Safe Schools Program. (It began as the Safe Schools Program for Gay and Lesbian Students, and the name was changed to the Safe Schools Program for LGBTQ Students in recent years.) Outside Massachusetts, other educators and activists used similar language in establishing some of the earliest programs focused on the needs of LGBTQ youth. Washington State's Safe Schools Coalition expanded from a Seattle-based group to a state-level program in 1993 to serve as a resource to educators who wanted to improve school environments for LGBTQ students. The Washington State coalition also provided (and continues to make available) research reports and other publications highlighting the issues affecting LGBTQ youth, which are used by educators, researchers, and advocates around the state and elsewhere. To reflect this broader focus, the organization is now called simply the "Safe Schools Coalition."[5]

In another example in which advocates have expressed the needs of LGBTQ students in terms of safety, in 2003 the New York City Department of Education, in cooperation with the Hetrick-Martin Institute (HMI), a social service agency dedicated to the needs of LGBTQ youth, expanded HMI's Harvey Milk High School into the first four-year school in the United States intended exclusively to serve LGBTQ students. Advocates for the school argued it would serve as a safe haven for young people who might not be or feel safe in other city schools. Although the school has had its detractors on both ends of the political spectrum— conservatives who disagree with the notion of public money used to fund a school exclusively for LGBTQ students and progressives who believe such a school sanctions segregation—its supporters have prevailed largely on the grounds that LGBTQ students need a "safe space" in which to learn.[6] As a description of the school on the Hetrick-Martin website still points out, it remains a necessary remedy to a less-than-ideal situation for LGBTQ students around the city: "In an ideal world, all students who are considered at risk would be safely integrated into all NYC public schools. But in the real world, at-risk students need a place like the Harvey Milk High School. HMHS is one of the many NYC small schools that provide safety, community, and high achievement for students not able to benefit from more traditional school environments."[7]

THREE MAIN CHARACTERISTICS OF SAFE SCHOOLS

Although the efforts of educators and advocates to make schools safer for LGBTQ students have taken many forms in different kinds of communities, nationally the "safe" paradigm has primarily centered on three components. Some schools have one or two of these components in place, and many have all three. But even schools with the full triad may be operating under a tacit agreement that "safe" is an acceptable standard for meeting the needs of their LGBTQ populations when they can and should be doing much more.

Antibullying Programs

Largely in response to several high-profile cases of peer-to-peer harassment publicized in the national media, some of which were associated with the suicides of students who were victimized, new or expanded antibullying policies have been implemented at all levels of government in the last several years. Some of these cases have involved LGBTQ-based harassment, including that of a high school freshman from a suburb of Buffalo, New York, who according to news reports was relentlessly harassed with antigay epithets and committed suicide in September 2011. Before taking his own life, he posted on the blog website Tumblr, "I always say how bullied I am, but no one listens. What do I have to do so people will listen?"[8]

Between 2008 and 2012, forty-nine of the fifty states either introduced or expanded antibullying legislation, and although most of these policies do not address the bullying of LGBTQ students specifically, they are often cited as evidence that schools and government are taking the needs of LGBTQ students seriously. Many of these bills use the language of safety in their names, such as Iowa's antibullying and antiharassment law, also known as the Iowa Safe Schools Law, which protects students from bullying and harassment based on "any of the following traits or characteristics: age, color, creed, national origin, race, religion, marital status, sex, sexual orientation, gender identity, physical attributes, physical or mental ability or disability, ancestry, political party preference, political belief, socioeconomic status, and familial status."[9] The United States Congress is currently considering the Safe Schools Improvement Act, a piece of antibullying legislation that would include specific protections for LGBTQ students.

The Gay, Lesbian and Straight Education Network (GLSEN), a national education and advocacy group that promotes improved school environments for LGBTQ students, strongly advocates such "enumeration"—the explicit listing of factors for which students might be subject to harassment or assault—for all antibullying policies. As a GLSEN policy statement explains, enumeration strengthens a school's capacity to protect not only LGBTQ students but any others who might be targeted:

Enumeration is essential to protecting as many students as possible from bullying and harassment. The strength of an enumerated law or policy is that it underscores those students who research shows are most likely to be bullied and harassed and least likely to be protected under non-enumerated antibullying laws and policies. While enumerated policies specifically highlight the most vulnerable students, they do not limit the policy only to those students. All students are protected, even if they do not fall into one of the enumerated categories. Enumeration that includes sexual orientation and gender identity removes any doubt that LGBT youth are protected from bullying and harassment.[10]

With enumeration, as GLSEN suggests, there is no ambiguity about the fact that anti-LGBTQ harassment and bullying are unacceptable—regardless of any religious or political beliefs that a student, teacher, administrator, parent, or community member might hold—and that educators have a non-negotiable responsibility to address it if it occurs. GLSEN's research has found that enumeration is associated with lower rates of victimization of LGBTQ students and a much higher incidence of teachers intervening when these students are targeted by their peers:

Enumeration provides teachers and school personnel with the tools they need to implement antibullying and harassment policies, making it easier for them to prevent bullying and intervene when incidents occur. Evidence shows that educators often do not recognize anti-LGBT bullying and harassment as unacceptable behavior. Sometimes they fail to respond to the problem due to prejudice or community pressure. When they can point to enumerated language that provides clear protection for LGBT students, they feel more comfortable enforcing the policy. Students in schools with enumerated policies reported that teachers intervene more than twice as often compared to students in schools with generic antibullying policies, and more than three times as often compared to students in schools with no policy at all.[11]

To the extent that antibullying programs and laws protect LGBTQ and other students from being taunted by their peers in school, online, or elsewhere, they clearly have contributed to important positive change. But some experts on gender- and sexuality-based harassment in schools have questioned whether the focus on bullying prevention has overgeneralized the various kinds of bias, discrimination, and harassment that specific subgroups of students, such as LGBTQ youth, experience. As Nan Stein, senior research scientist at the Wellesley Centers for Women, has noted, "When schools put these new anti-bullying laws and policies into practice, the policies are often overly broad and arbitrary. . . [and] sometimes egregious behaviors are framed by school personnel as bullying, when in fact they may constitute illegal sexual or gender harassment or even criminal hazing or assault."[12] Moreover, antibullying policies, if they represent the *only* action school administrators take to support LGBTQ students, can create a false impression that the full range of these students' needs is being met.

LGBTQ "Safe Zones"

Another way in which "safe" language is central to schools' efforts to improve climates for LGBTQ students is the designation within many school buildings of "safe zones," often indicated by stickers on the classroom or office doors of individual teachers, counselors, administrators, or staff members who choose to use them. These "safe zone" or "safe space" stickers, which first started appearing in the 1990s and of which there are many versions, serve an important symbolic function in that they announce to students without the need for any discussion that these educators are, in one way or another, LGBTQ-friendly. A safe zone sticker on an educator's door can imply any number of things: that they will challenge anti-LGBTQ language and harassment when it occurs; they are open to the discussion of LGBTQ issues in the context of classwork or just in conversation; they might be a safe person to whom an LGBTQ student could "come out"; and in some cases, that the educator is lesbian, gay, bisexual, transgender, queer, or questioning.

Between 2010 and 2013, GLSEN took the idea of safe zone stickers to the next level by sending a "safe space kit" to every public middle and high school in the United States. In addition to ten safe zone stickers, the kit included a safe space poster as well as a "Guide to Being an Ally to LGBT Students," which offered strategies for supporting LGBTQ students and teaching about anti-LGBTQ harassment and violence.[13]

Several research studies, including GLSEN's biennial National School Climate Survey, which draws on the responses of roughly 7,900 students nationwide, have demonstrated that the safe space campaign, like enumerated antibullying policies, makes a tremendous difference in LGBTQ students' perceptions that their schools are safe and that their teachers are adults they can trust. Unfortunately, only about one-fourth (26 percent) of the students participating in the latest GLSEN survey said they had seen any safe zone stickers in their schools, but those who had felt significantly more positive attitudes toward their teachers and other school staff than their peers who had not. Whereas about half of GLSEN's survey participants who had not seen a safe zone sticker or poster had an adult at school with whom they felt comfortable talking about LGBTQ issues, nearly three-quarters of students who had seen the stickers had such an adult in their school.

Gay-Straight Alliances

Finally, the notion of safe space has also been central to the emergence of gay-straight alliances (GSAs), extracurricular organizations in which LGBTQ young people and their allies support one another, plan educational programming for the school community about LGBTQ issues, and sometimes just "hang out" in an atmosphere where it is okay to be gay, lesbian, bisexual, transgender, queer, questioning, or even straight.

Widely considered the precursor to the GSA movement in the United States, Project 10 in the Los Angeles Unified School District began in 1984 and continues today. Project 10 is a broad-based program that includes many components associated with the psychological and academic well-being of LGBTQ students, but one of its primary missions has always been to ensure "on-campus groups that are safe zones for LGBT students" in Los Angeles schools.[14]

GSAs proliferated around Massachusetts starting in the 1990s when the groundbreaking Safe Schools Program began providing seed money and educational and technical support to students and educators who wanted to start them. From the start, GSAs have been controversial in many of the communities in which they have been introduced, where conservative critics have argued that they raise issues pertaining to sexuality that are better left to families and religious communities. (See, for example, the profile of Missouri's Nixa High School in chapter 3.) The teachers, administrators, and students who have started GSAs have often countered such criticism with the argument that their primary purpose is to provide much-needed "safe space" for LGBTQ students who might not otherwise feel safe in their schools.

Although far too many schools still do not have gay-straight alliances, these groups have grown exponentially over the last decade. The latest National School Climate Survey conducted by GLSEN found that about half of students surveyed indicated there were GSAs in their schools.[15] Many GSAs also register with GLSEN, and at last count the national organization had well over four thousand such groups on its national roster. Whereas at one time GSAs were geographically concentrated in traditionally liberal bastions such as California, New York City, and the Boston area, now they can be found in schools in all fifty states. In many places, GSAs do in fact serve a crucial function as safe havens, offering to LGBTQ young people the only place in their schools where they feel comfortable enough to talk openly and be themselves.

There is overwhelming evidence that gay-straight alliances make a tremendous difference in the school lives of LGBTQ students. GLSEN's most recent survey found that students who attend schools with GSAs are less likely to feel unsafe for reasons associated with their sexual orientation, are less likely to hear homophobic language regularly at school, report considerably higher levels of peer acceptance, and generally feel more connected to their school communities.[16] Another study associated GSAs with feelings of both personal and institutional "empowerment" for

LGBTQ students—for example, feeling comfortable holding a same-sex girlfriend's or boyfriend's hand in the hallway or having the confidence to work toward change in school and government policies.[17]

Like an antibullying program, however, the presence of a GSA, while essential, can also allow school officials who feel the pressures of competing priorities (such as raising test scores), or who fear controversy around LGBTQ-themed programming, to claim that the issue has been "covered" and therefore no further action is required. As long as LGBTQ students and their allies have a place to go once a week and a faculty advisor to talk to, school decision makers may not see the need for these young people to be supported all day, every day at school. They can fail to examine curriculum, athletics, extracurricular clubs, or other aspects of school life from which students may still feel excluded.

SAFETY FIRST

Let me be *very* clear: "safe schools" policies and programs, enumerated antibullying initiatives, LGBTQ safe zone stickers and posters, and gay-straight alliances all make a critical, life-saving difference in the school experiences of LGBTQ students. Given LGBTQ youths' persistently disproportionate risk for harassment, feeling unsafe at school, substance abuse, and suicide, safety is a critical baseline from which all subsequent work must follow.[18] The educators and advocates who built the early successes of the LGBTQ student rights movement understood this. As a result, many schools are much, much safer places for LGBTQ students than they were thirty, twenty, even ten years ago. And it has become clear to more and more people that those schools that still offer no basic protections or safe space to LGBTQ students need to change immediately.

Yet the notion of GSAs as a "safe space" or certain teachers' rooms as "safe zones," as well as the framing of initiatives to benefit LGBTQ students as "safe schools" programming, raises a number of crucial questions as educators and advocates look toward what must happen next to build on these successes. If a certain place in the school is designated as a safe space, what does that say about the rest of the building? If certain educators are seen as "safe" for students to talk to about issues that are central to their lives, what about the others? Does a school administration have a responsibility to ensure that LGBTQ students feel supported by *all* their teachers in *every* learning space in the building, not just treated with mere "tolerance" by the majority? Is safety the only thing to which LGBTQ students are entitled at school? What about the skills and knowledge they need to be effective, engaged members of their society *as LGBTQ youth*? Finally, are LGBTQ students a monolithic group with one basic common need: safety? What differences exist among various subgroups within the LGBTQ student population—boys and girls, transgender students, LGBTQ students of color—and the way they experience the school climate and programs? What would an optimal education for all these young people look like?

A CRITICAL MOMENT

While much remains to be done, our country is arguably at a watershed moment with regard to both LGBTQ rights and shifting public attitudes about LGBTQ issues. The right to marry for all couples, regardless of their sex, is now the law of the land in all fifty states. Perhaps even more significantly, the recent changes in marriage law have occurred with far less public outcry than would have been imaginable even ten years ago. Although there are still conservative activists around the country working to overturn the Supreme Court's decision legalizing same-sex marriage and to challenge other LGBTQ rights—and these are more prevalent in some geographical areas than others—the chances that such challenges will ultimately succeed seem to be growing increasingly slim.

One of the reasons for this wave of policy change may be the dramatic shift in public attitudes about homosexuality and LGBTQ rights that has occurred in recent years. Whereas through the late 1980s only about a third of participants in Gallup's annual polls said they believed gay or lesbian relations between consenting adults should be legal, that number rose to two-thirds by 2014. On the issue of same-sex marriage, the changes have been even more dramatic: as recently as 1996, only 27 percent of Americans said they believed marriages between same-sex couples should be recognized by law as valid, but 55 percent approved of their legal recognition by 2014 (and a 2015 CBS News poll prior to the Supreme Court's ruling found this number to be as high as 60 percent).[19]

Although popular media still depict heterosexuality and traditional expressions of gender as the norm, images of same-sex relationships and LGBTQ identities are now more common in mainstream popular culture than ever before. And while LGBTQ people of color and transgender people are still sparsely represented in the media, they are certainly more visible than they were a decade or two ago (the celebrity of openly gay black NFL player Michael Sam and the Amazon web series *Transparent* being two such examples). Moreover, the wide availability of information and resources about LGBTQ issues and identities online has contributed further to the emergence of a new age that might have seemed unimaginable even twenty years ago.

Within this larger cultural context in which attitudes about LGBTQ people and identities have shifted so favorably and so quickly, progress has also been made on the school front, but much more slowly and inconsistently. GLSEN's latest National School Climate Survey showed that significantly fewer students hear homophobic remarks "frequently" or "often" in their schools than did at the beginning of the century, but this was still a problem for about two-thirds of the students polled. The percentage of students reporting that they have a GSA in their school was higher in the latest survey than in all prior survey years but still hovered around the 50 percent mark, indicating that nearly half the students polled still do not have access to a GSA. The percentage of students reporting representation of LGBTQ people and issues in their school curricula also was higher than ever in the latest survey; nevertheless, four out of five students still said there was no positive representation of LGBTQ people or issues in any of their classes, and less than half (44 percent) said they had access to LGBTQ-related information in their school library.[20]

Despite the progress that's been made, unwelcoming school climates continue to take a toll on the physical, emotional, and academic well-being of LGBTQ students. Nearly one-third of the students in the last GLSEN survey said they had missed at least one entire day of school in the past month because they felt unsafe or uncomfortable, and one in ten missed four or more days. LGBTQ students who had experienced high levels of victimization were significantly more likely than other LGBTQ youth to miss school because of feeling unsafe, have lower grade point averages, report that they did not plan to go to college, and suffer from depression and low self-esteem.[21]

Finally, progress on LGBTQ issues seems to have come further for some students than others depending on geography and on their specific identities under the LGBTQ umbrella. Students in the South and Midwest regions of the United States reported the highest levels of harassment, perceived lack of safety, and anti-LGBTQ language in their schools on the 2013 survey, and they were the least likely to report access to GSAs, LGBTQ-inclusive curricula, and teachers they felt they could talk to about LGBTQ issues. (Whereas 60 percent of students responding to the survey from the Northeast said their schools had GSAs, only 33 percent of students in the South said so.) Moreover, transgender students in the GLSEN survey reported the highest levels of harassment and the lowest levels of perceived safety among all participating students, and transgender identities tend to be the least represented in curricula, library resources, and other school materials and programs.[22]

This larger context of progress in some, but not all, aspects of society and of schooling has led me to the three related premises on which this book is based:

- Safety is an essential baseline for schools' ability to meet the needs of LGBTQ students effectively and has served as a critical foundation for efforts to introduce policies and programs at all levels of government to benefit LGBTQ students, *but it is not a sufficient goal in itself.*
- Considerable progress has been made in recent decades on LGBTQ issues in schools, but inconsistencies with regard to geographical location, identity categories within the LGBTQ spectrum, and other factors have created *inequities that are unacceptable.*
- Recent political progress and shifts in public attitudes about LGBTQ issues suggest an opportune time for educators and policy makers to move beyond "safe" and create schools that *affirm LGBTQ*

students and integrate respect for LGBTQ identities through multiple aspects of school life.

A NEW PARADIGM: BEYOND "SAFE"

If the safe spaces represented by antibullying policies, LGBTQ safe zones, and gay-straight alliances were viewed not as ends in themselves but merely as foundations for schools that are supportive, inclusive, and affirming of all LGBTQ students—all day and every day—what might these "new and improved" schools look like? And, perhaps even more importantly, how would we get there? What steps might educators take to bring their schools to the next level?

The chapters that follow map out eight aspects of such a vision and profile district leaders, school administrators, classroom teachers, counselors, and others who embody each aspect in their day-to-day practice. Working in various contexts that pose different sets of challenges—from urban poverty to political or religious conservatism to the age of the students they serve—all of the educators interviewed for this book are engaged *in a process* of moving their work on LGBTQ issues to a higher level. Some are further along in this process than others. Yet despite the limitations these educators face, each is engaged in practices that show not only that we *should* do more for the LGBTQ youth in our schools, but that we *can* push toward a new standard of practice, beyond keeping students safe, even in schools where many might not think it possible.

The classroom is in many respects the heart of school life, yet for the vast majority of students—even those attending ostensibly safe schools—it is also a place in which LGBTQ people and identities are never mentioned. Chapter 1, "Bringing the Conversation into the Classroom," draws primarily on the work of two teachers who engage high school students in critical discussions about gender and sexual orientation. Contrary to the all-too-common practice of having a gay-straight alliance be the only space in the school where words such as *transgender* or *lesbian* are spoken, these educators bring LGBTQ issues directly into their classrooms. The chapter also profiles a statewide curricular initiative from which educators all over the country can acquire ideas for making their classes LGBTQ-inclusive.

Ideally, schools and districts would not implement curricular programs in isolation; they would integrate them in a comprehensive way to create an overall climate of inclusiveness that is palpable in every hallway and classroom of the school. Chapter 2, "Transforming the Building," profiles a suburban New York–area school that has done just that and exemplifies how LGBTQ issues can be integrated across multiple aspects of school life. Certainly, the school's location in the nation's largest metropolitan area lends itself to a relatively hospitable environment for LGBTQ issues. Nevertheless, one factor that makes this school exceptional is that it is not a high school, but a middle school serving students in grades six through eight. Countering the common misconception that students in the middle grades are too young to have serious discussions about issues such as transgender identity or the LGBTQ rights movement, the teachers, administrators, staff, and students interviewed for this chapter exemplify how, as one staff member put it, "it's just part of what we do here." Especially important at this school is the leadership provided by a Spanish teacher who also serves as the school's GSA advisor and facilitates professional development sessions for faculty, both in formalized group settings and through one-on-one coaching, to help teachers integrate LGBTQ-inclusive content with their own curricular goals.

As indicated previously, gay-straight alliances are life-saving programs in schools that provide LGBTQ young people and their allies a "safe space" to meet once a week or so. Chapter 3, "Turning Adversity into Activism," focuses on schools that have taken their GSAs to the next level, largely by necessity. These schools in Missouri and Utah illustrate how educators working in politically or religiously conservative areas have special responsibilities to their LGBTQ students. The GSA advisors in these two schools have helped students develop a stance of resistance not only to homophobia and transphobia in their schools, but also to government policies and religious doctrines in the communities surrounding them that threaten the rights and dignity of LGBTQ people.

Just as it is important to affirm the aspects of students' identities that relate to their being lesbian, gay, bisexual, transgender, queer, or questioning, it is equally important to remember that these identities exist in a broader context that also includes issues such as race, ethnicity, and socioeconomics. Chapter 4, "Tapping into Community Assets," examines the work of educators in a high-poverty urban school in Hawaii that serves a large population of immigrant students from Asian and Pacific Islander families. For these educators, supporting their students also means helping them negotiate what it means to be LGBTQ within families and communities in which nontraditional expressions of gender and sexuality may prompt cultural conflict, and to see their place in a larger culture that often represents LGBTQ identity primarily as white and middle-class. The work in this school shows how role modeling and media literacy can be especially important for helping LGBTQ youth of color develop strong, confident identities *as LGBTQ youth of color*.

Among all students under the LGBTQ umbrella, transgender students are often the most underserved by their schools: they face the highest rate of harassment, see little or no representation of their identities in curricula, and face daily indignities related to everything from locker room and bathroom usage to the use of their preferred names and pronouns. Even in schools with strong GSAs and related programming, transgender students can feel excluded and marginalized. Moreover, transgender students often face high levels of parental rejection, making school acceptance and education all the more important. Chapter 5, "Respecting the 'T' in LGBTQ," looks at school practices specifically intended to make schools more welcoming for transgender students at three levels: district policy, building-level leadership, and the day-to-day experiences of teachers, students, and families.

GSAs are often cited by researchers—and by youth themselves— as places in which LGBTQ students can talk openly without fear of being judged, rejected, or ostracized. But in many schools, the GSA isn't the only place in which students can talk about the challenges— or the joys—they experience being lesbian, gay, bisexual, transgender, queer, or questioning. Chapter 6, "Opening Up Spaces for Discussion," profiles an LGBTQ-specific counseling group in Georgia, a book club centered largely on LGBTQ-themed titles in Florida, and a California health teacher who serves in more informal ways as a trusted mentor and resource to LGBTQ students. Collectively, these educators and programs illustrate the value of having many spaces in the school building, beyond the GSA, where LGBTQ youth can talk about their feelings and experiences.

Most of the work profiled in chapters 1 through 6 takes place in high schools or, in the case of Jericho, New York, middle school. Secondary schools, however, are not the only schools that need to move beyond the "safe" paradigm. Chapter 7, "Making It Elementary," profiles three programs—one developed by a national LGBTQ rights organization, one by the parent of a gender-nonconforming child in Washington State, and another by a teacher conducting her own classroom-based research in Chicago—to address issues related to gender and sexuality with elementary school students. Recognizing that children's prejudices about gender and LGBTQ individuals are formed early, the educators interviewed for this chapter use everything from children's books to visual art to lining up for recess as teaching tools that help students think critically, in age-appropriate ways, about prevailing stereotypes and their effects.

If the educators profiled in chapters 1 through 7 are implementing practices to which school leaders who want to make their schools more than "safe" might aspire, where does this process begin? Chapter 8, "Where Do You Start? Beginning with Core Values—but Not Ending There," illustrates how progress toward many of the changes proposed in this book can begin by tapping into core values and common beliefs on which an entire community already agrees. This chapter includes a case study of a high school in a politically conservative suburb of Indianapolis where educators have successfully justified the creation of a more LGBTQ-inclusive climate on the grounds that the district's mission statement, strategic plan, and established policies already require it. Although this school has room to grow toward integrating LGBTQ issues across all aspects of school life (as the superintendent and building-level administrators and teachers acknowledge), educators there have made great strides in a relatively short time largely by drawing on broader themes and district trends.

Finally, the afterword invites readers to think even beyond the notion of "better" schools for LGBTQ youth toward an ideal educational experience for these students. Drawing on the progress outlined in the previous eight chapters, this afterword looks toward a future in which "safe spaces" will be a given and LGBTQ issues will be woven into the fabric of school life.

ABOUT THIS BOOK

The idea for this book sprung from my belief—based on years of work in schools as a teacher, researcher, and teacher educator—that for every educator doing innovative, "outside the box" work to support LGBTQ students, there are about a dozen more who want to do the same but need ideas and guidance. My hope is that teachers, administrators, counselors, and other education professionals (as well as those studying to enter a school-related field) will learn from the colleagues they read about here not only what is possible but also how to make it happen, even in the face of considerable obstacles.

Since my purpose in this book is to report on a broad range of work going on in schools across the country rather than to investigate a specific research question, I have approached collecting the information herein as an education journalist as opposed to a qualitative researcher (although other work I have published has been more qualitative in nature). I sought out information about outstanding teachers and schools from a variety of sources: professional organizations, colleagues, database searches, news reports, even word of mouth. I gathered information through a combination of in-person, telephone, and e-mail interviews (sometimes using multiple methods for the same interviewee). The educators I spoke with often referred me to colleagues in their schools, whom I contacted to round out the portrait of work going on there. In many cases, educators referred me to current and former students, who were also interviewed either in person or by telephone, or answered questions over e-mail. (Some were interviewed in multiple ways.)

Because readers may wish to learn more about the programming in some of the schools they read about here, the names of all schools and educators quoted in this book are real. Students, however, are either unnamed or are given pseudonyms to protect their anonymity (and, for consistency, I have used pseudonyms both for current students and for former students, even those who are now well into adulthood). Except where indicated, the comments of people quoted in these chapters are based on communication with me directly for the purposes of this book.

In addition, it should be noted that the subtitle of this book is "Better Schools for LGBTQ Students" for the sake of brevity and clarity. This is not intended to exclude all the other LGBTQ-positive work going on in schools, such as support for students whose parents might be LGBTQ, support for straight allies in student groups (e.g., gay-straight alliances), or efforts to teach students to be better allies to their LGBTQ peers, all of which are also represented.

The ideas presented here and the examples of schools and educators that are implementing them by no means constitute a comprehensive list of all the possibilities. Other creative educators are no doubt doing outstanding work in other schools not represented in these pages. Moreover, the schools profiled are all works in progress, the educators all doing good work but striving to do better. But they share a belief that "safe is not enough" for their students, and their collective efforts help point the way toward what I hope can be a new standard for schools that are more than just safe—not only for LGBTQ youth, but for all children and adolescents.

CHAPTER 1

Bringing the Conversation into the Classroom

I T IS DIFFICULT TO IMAGINE any serious effort to reform schooling that does not involve changing the content of what is taught in classrooms. Common Core, Race to the Top, No Child Left Behind, and all other federal efforts to improve schools in recent memory have trickled their way down to the classroom in profound ways and have greatly influenced curricular decisions and teaching methods, often beyond the point of what is in the best interest of students, in order to raise test scores.

By contrast, efforts to improve schools for LGBTQ students, as important a difference as they have made in the last several decades, have rarely involved change at the classroom level. Despite the growth of gay-straight alliances around the country, improved policies to combat anti-LGBTQ bullying, and other reforms, LGBTQ-inclusive curriculum continues to lag behind these other measures. The latest GLSEN School Climate Survey indicated that fewer than one in five students report any representation of LGBTQ people or issues in any of their classes.[1] Even in schools in relatively progressive communities, LGBTQ-inclusive curriculum remains rare.

This chapter begins with profiles of two curricular initiatives at the classroom level, one of which was implemented well over a decade ago. Around the turn of the last century, curriculum representation of LGBTQ issues was less common than it is now, even in schools that were ostensibly "safe" for LGBTQ students. As education scholar Arthur

Lipkin wrote in his 1999 volume *Understanding Homosexuality: Changing Schools*: "Many schools still bend over backward to distinguish between acceptable discrimination policies and forbidden classroom lessons. For instance, despite unanimously voted protections for homosexual students in one Maryland County, officials would not permit displays of gay-related books or talks by homosexual speakers and classes. 'That would be proselytizing,' declared the superintendent."[2]

So in 2002, when Amherst, Massachusetts, high school English teacher Sara Barber-Just designed a curriculum for a low-residency master's degree program she was completing at Vermont's Goddard College in LGBTQ literature, she wasn't sure it would ever see the light of day: "What I really wanted to do—but I thought 'nobody can do this,' was teach a whole course in gay and lesbian literature. Everything I'd heard—and everything I still hear—is that it's too controversial."

Barber-Just completed a course outline for one of her graduate classes in Goddard's social justice education program, and she received permission to teach a pilot version of the class in a ten-student alternative learning program at Amherst High School beginning in 2002. Since the course was not part of the regular curriculum, Barber-Just taught it without pay for two years, taking her official position and salary down to 90 percent so that she could make room for it in her schedule. Even for the alternative learning setting, Barber-Just thought it was important to design the course in an ironclad way, one that demonstrated it had many of the same goals as a more traditional English course. She organized it chronologically, like a traditional American literature class, focusing on how the LGBTQ-themed literature illustrated changing attitudes and social mores over time: "I thought conservatively at first: 'What does an American literature course look like in high school?' If I ever had to present this to someone who wouldn't understand it, I wanted it to look like a regular American literature class."

After overwhelmingly positive reviews of the pilot course in the alternative learning program, Barber-Just proposed the class as an elective in Amherst High School's regular English language arts program. Following a unanimous vote from the English department and enthusiastic approval by the school board, the course was added to Amherst's schedule as an elective in 2004 and quickly grew to four sections, with a total enrollment of about one hundred students. Since then, the class has grown even more and has become one of the most popular courses in the school's English department, enrolling about one hundred fifty students per year in six sections. On several occasions when more students enrolled than Barber-Just could accommodate in her schedule, another teacher took over a few sections. Barber-Just now estimates that about half of every graduating senior class has taken the course by the time they graduate.

LGBTQ LITERATURE AT AMHERST HIGH SCHOOL

Still rooted in its original conception as a traditionally organized American literature course, LGBTQ Literature (the name was changed in the 2014–2015 school year to reflect the full spectrum of sexual orientation and gender identity) begins with an examination of classic American literature by authors such as Willa Cather and Walt Whitman, widely considered by many scholars to have had same-sex attractions that come through in their work in both overt and oblique ways.[3] Some scholars, for example, believe that Willa Cather's male protagonists are in subtextual ways modeled on herself, including their attraction to women. As Barber-Just explains, "In a lot of Willa Cather's novels, a male character is in love with a woman he can't have, and that woman loves a different kind of man." (See exhibit 1.1 in appendix A for a recent syllabus from Barber-Just's course.)

In addition to the chronological survey of literature written by LGBTQ authors and addressing LGBTQ themes, students complete a media analysis project in which they compare how LGBTQ individuals were depicted by Hollywood in the twentieth century (as illustrated in the documentary film *The Celluloid Closet*) to LGBTQ representations in film, television, and music today.[4] (See exhibit 1.2 in appendix A.) As Cleo, a student in Barber-Just's class in 2014, describes in a reflection written for the course, "After *The Celluloid Closet*, I started seeing gay subtexts everywhere. No, I couldn't confirm that they were gay subtexts, but it made the world feel a little less straight."

Studying LGBTQ identity development models, Barber-Just and her students use the various developmental stages presented in these models as lenses through which to view certain characters in the literature they read. (For example, how does James Baldwin's *Giovanni's Room* exemplify the "identity confusion" stage in Richard Troiden's developmental model?[5]) Until recently, the course did not include a full-length work with a transgender protagonist. Instead, students discussed transgender identity using a variety of shorter source texts: "I didn't have a whole book that focused on transgender issues, but it ended up having just as much time as the other issues," Barber-Just says. "We read sections of Janet Mock's book *Redefining Realness*, interviews with her and with Laverne Cox; we watched the Dutch film *I Am a Girl*. One day we watched the whole Caitlyn Jenner interview [on ABC]. I've also had a panel of transgender and gender-queer people come in during the last few weeks of the class." (See the profile of Janet Mock's alma mater, Honolulu's Farrington High School, in chapter 4.) Barber-Just also plans to add Amy Ellis Nutt's book *Becoming Nicole*, which tells the story of twins, one of whom is transgender, to the syllabus.[6]

Studying *Giovanni's Room* and more contemporary pieces by LGBTQ people of color, as well as the depictions of LGBTQ people of color in the media, Barber-Just's class also has a strong intersectional component, something she says her students have encouraged her to expand. The concept of *intersectionality*, which addresses how various aspects of identity such as LGBTQ and racial identity interconnect in people's lives, was a focus Barber-Just says she added several years ago at students' suggestion: "Kids had that language [such as the term *intersectionality*] before me, and it's really helped me think about the books we're reading. From the beginning, the kids were always ahead of me."[7]

Students can also take the class for AP credit by reading two additional, more difficult works of literature. More than half the students complete the AP project, and books for AP credit have included Alice Walker's *The Color Purple*, Leslie Feinberg's *Stone Butch Blues*, Jeffrey Eugenides' *Middlesex*, Alison Bechdel's *Fun Home*, Charles Rice-Gonzales's *Chulito*, and Sri Lankan author Shyam Selvadurai's *Funny Boy*.

In addition to growing class enrollment, the demographics of students taking the course have also changed. "It used to be all queer youth, mostly girls. A lot of boys take it now," Barber-Just says. "Sometimes no one ever comes out [as LGBTQ]; other times I've had like eight kids come out." About 30 percent of students at the school are from immigrant families representing a variety of nationalities and religions, virtually all of which have been represented in the class: "There's no stigma attached to it now. Religious kids take it. The demographics are just like any other course."

One possible downside to these changing demographics, Barber-Just adds, is that the course is no longer the haven it once was for LGBTQ youth, but perhaps the benefits of the course's popularity with a larger population outweigh the costs: "It's much more empowering [for LGBTQ students] to see their straight and cisgender classmates grow so much and be so supportive."*

Former Students Speak to the Impact of the Course

In 2014, Barber-Just was one of four recipients of Williams College's George Olmsted Jr. Class of 1924 Prize for Excellence in Secondary School Teaching. She had been nominated by a 2014 Williams graduate, a former student in her LGBTQ literature class, who said in a news article following the award announcement, "It [the course] forced me to look at my own stereotypes and prejudices."[8]

A more recent graduate, Robert, from the AHS class of 2015, credits the course with having inspired him to be a social justice educator like Barber-Just in his own future career. He reported:

> I am in the middle of my first week at Brandeis University with the intention of becoming a high school English teacher, largely due to the influence of Ms. Barber-Just and LGBTQ Lit. Ms. Barber-Just

---

* The term *cisgender* is often used as a counterpart to *transgender* and refers to a gender identity in accordance with one's sex assigned at birth.

used the stories of Willa Cather, Oscar Wilde, Rita Mae Brown, James Baldwin, and other fantastic authors to inspire truly powerful discussions. Nothing was off limits: #blacklivesmatter, Laverne Cox, the Kinsey scale, and misogyny in Hip-Hop all came up in classroom discussions. Ms. Barber-Just guided fluid and relevant dialogues that engaged nearly every student. Students who never participated in other classes came to LGBTQ Lit ready to read and dialogue.

She taught me that gender and sexuality exist on a spectrum. She taught terms such as *pansexual* and *cisgender*. Ms. Barber-Just also supplemented the core texts with articles and videos to provide historical context for the authors and their stories and a framework for critical analysis. She embraced the intersectionality of these stories with questions such as, "Why doesn't Rita Mae Brown mention the race of any characters? What do you think of this color-blind mentality?" She encouraged nitty-gritty embarrassing questions such as, "How should I address a transgender person if I am not sure of their gender?" Instead of falling into the trap of many English teachers, of dealing with the texts abstractly, Ms. Barber-Just made the stories relevant by drawing connections to our Amherst Regional High School experience. She gave every student a voice.[9]

Another recent graduate, Stephan, said in the final course reflection he wrote for the class:

This class has really opened my eyes, as I knew it would. I've always been of the opinion that good classes teach you valuable material while great classes alter your perception altogether. I can't say that many classes have done this for me . . . This trimester has not only given me a peek into the nuances of the homosexual subculture, but it let me actually read the accounts of gay writers who either struggled with gayness or bore their homosexuality with pride. It is inspiring to see how the culture of prejudice changed from book to book and decade to decade. From *A Lost Lady*, where everything was subtly implied, to *Giovanni's Room*, riddled with self-hatred, *Rubyfruit Jungle*, which doesn't take any crap, finally culminating in *The Hours*, in which we finally see a gay writer able to settle in and write like any straight writer, accepted.

Even well over a decade after Barber-Just began teaching the course, few schools have followed suit to include a course specifically centered on LGBTQ-related literature. Yet as Cheryl, a student in Barber-Just's first section of the course in 2002, attests, breaking the silence on LGBTQ issues in the classroom can have a lasting impact on students. Cheryl shared the following reflections, which speak to the way a course like Barber-Just's could help break through the silence pervading a student's high school experience:

I was one of the ten students in the pilot class of Sara Barber-Just's Gay & Lesbian Literature course during the spring of 2002. I had just turned 18 years old and it was nearing the end of my final year of high school. Despite attacks of senioritis, I rushed excitedly to school each day for the 7:35 a.m. first bell because I couldn't wait for my A-period class with Ms. Just.

I had realized I was gay three years before at age fifteen and came out to my family (parents and brother) a year later after I started dating my first real girlfriend. My parents—liberal academics—didn't disown me, love me less, or even treat me differently, but my declaration upset them and created significant tension. We didn't talk about my sexual orientation or my dating life. It was too embarrassing and confusing for all of us. And my parents didn't know if they should take what I had told them seriously. Meanwhile, I was exhilarated, but also scared by the thrill of first loves, by the secrecy and taboo of lesbian cultures, by the danger and daring of being out in high school. I jumped at the chance to take Sara's new course when she invited me to join it after we had gotten to know each other in another course, Women in Literature.

Sara's class was a real live oasis in a time when my gay friends and I were searching desperately for community and information at oasismag.com, a site for LGBT teens on the nascent internet. It was sheer pleasure to enter a space each morning devoted to gay culture and facilitated by a wonderful young out lesbian teacher, who shared freely about her own journey and her present life with her partner, which sounded like an idyllic fantasy. Just being in that room already felt almost too good to be true.

But the course itself turned out to be a real bonus, and I still carry with me much of what I learned there. We read Willa Cather, James Baldwin, Rita Mae Brown, Michael Cunningham, and others. I discovered with awe the rich history of gay literati and felt a kinship with these intellectuals and their narratives. I found out about lesbian subtexts. I learned about Stonewall and the politics of gay liberation. We read contemporaneous arguments in the lesbian and gay community regarding the desirability of legalizing gay marriage—did we really want any part of a fundamentally flawed, patriarchal institution?—way before the rise of a national "marriage equality" movement.

There was no pressure for us students to come out to our classmates or share personal stories about LGBT experience, and I don't remember this being a big or important part of the class. We didn't want to talk about ourselves because we were shy teenagers and we didn't need to because we were already reading, discussing, and learning from other people's gay experiences every day. The insides of books and articles were safe, while also stimulating subjects of debate and objects of analysis.

And this was the case not only in our classroom, at least for me. My brother and I were used to telling our parents about what we were learning in school over the dinner table. Sharing discussions from my Gay & Lesbian Literature course allowed me to begin talking about gay identity with my parents, broaching an uncomfortable subject, and educating them while I was educated myself.[10]

SETTING LGBTQ ISSUES IN A LARGER CONTEXT

While Barber-Just's course in LGBTQ literature remains a rare example of a high school class focused exclusively on LGBTQ subject matter, New York City public school teacher Maggie Chesnut addresses LGBTQ identities and issues in the broader context of struggles for civil rights in a social studies course called "Movement Building." In the class, which Chesnut has taught as a yearlong social studies elective primarily for seniors (though a few juniors and sophomores have also taken it), students explore the histories of various social movements and the strategies various groups across history have used to effect change. Chesnut developed the course while teaching at the High School for Health Professions and Human Services in Manhattan.

Chesnut's course uses the concept of identity as a lens through which students view various social movements, and students are encouraged to think about the similarities and differences among various identity-based struggles throughout history. Taking this intersectional approach, Chesnut explains, helps students view the struggle for LGBTQ rights not as an isolated series of events but as one aspect of a broader movement for equality in the United States. In the most recent section of the course, students learned about the 1969 rebellion at the Stonewall Inn in New York City, widely regarded as the pivotal moment that led to the contemporary LGBTQ civil rights movement, and considered its possible connections to more recent uprisings in Baltimore and Ferguson, Missouri, protesting the treatment of black youth by police officers (and the deaths of young men in some of these encounters). As Chesnut recalls:

We talked about identity-focused organizing versus organizing around a specific goal and how each affects who feels included and excluded in the movement. We compared the coverage of the riots in Baltimore to the original coverage of the Stonewall riots and considered whether history books would eventually see the Baltimore and Ferguson riots as the beginnings of a movement the way the Stonewall riots are now understood. We studied mass incarceration through the book *The New Jim Crow* and then looked at organizations like "Break Out!" that are focusing on the criminalization of black transgender youth. In our "Breaking Down Gender" unit, we looked at how norms for gender and sexuality are different in cultures around the world and at different points in history.[11]

Just as the LGBTQ rights movement exists within a larger struggle for equal rights, LGBTQ identities exist not in isolation but in the context of an individual's race, gender, and other factors. Like Barber-Just, Chesnut encourages students to make personal connections to their course material through exercises that illustrate how various identity-related factors intersect in their own lives. Chesnut begins the class with an "identity chart" activity (drawn from the *Facing History and Ourselves* resource guide) in which students depict on a circular chart the various factors that influence their identities.[12] In modeling this exercise for students, Chesnut "comes out" as a "queer, white, antiracist female educator," and this disclosure prompts students to consider how factors such as race, gender, and sexual orientation influence their own lives. Since most of the class in Manhattan was black or Latino, and many were from immigrant families from various places such as West Africa, the Caribbean, Mexico, and Bangladesh, the identity charts students produced captured the rich diversity of the class. Even though only a few students identified as LGBTQ, Chesnut says the broader discussion of identity encouraged all students to feel safe "coming out" about their own experiences, whatever they might be: "I structured the class so that there was a lot of space for them to share their personal stories—a lot of chances for them to connect to the material. It was really relevant to who they were and their experience of the world."

Chesnut followed up the introductory identity work with units on "Eugenics and Scientific Racism," "Breaking Down Gender," "Feminism and the Media," and "LGBT History." The racism unit, Chesnut says, was extremely popular with students because "it was cathartic to have at least a partial explanation for the way racism has become embedded into our society." Chesnut adds that the unit "Breaking Down Gender" was the most challenging and led to the most student resistance, "but by the end, a lot of them were starting to question things like sex-segregated bathrooms, sports teams, and identifying gender on official IDs. Through heated discussions, most of the class came to the conclusion that the gender binary is constructed, and that a spectrum of gender expression should be respected."

Drawing on the fact that many students were from families with a recent history of immigration, Chesnut's gender unit also included an assignment that required students to research gender customs in different countries. This project encouraged students to think more broadly about gender, and students became particularly interested in how the concept of gender was understood in their families' countries of origin:

> I found that this was a successful way to drive home how gender and sexuality are constructed by asking students to research "gender customs" around the world. The fact that a handful of countries even legally recognize a third gender blew their minds and made them start questioning US policies around gender, like whether we should even have to identify gender on our IDs like drivers' licenses and passports. One student argued that the only reason we would have to identify our gender would be to oppress certain genders, and there would be greater justice in leaving it off entirely. Other students seemed excited to learn about how gender is perceived in the countries their parents or grandparents were born in. One of my students with Dominican heritage was particularly fascinated with the guevedoche people from the Dominican Republic. (The guevedoches are intersex people who are born with female traits and then develop male secondary sex characteristics during puberty.[13])

For the LGBT history unit, Chesnut (like Barber-Just) moves students through chronologically, beginning in the 1800s with what were called "romantic friendships," studies the homophile movement of the mid-1900s, teaches about the Stonewall rebellion, then discusses the evolution of the post-Stonewall LGBTQ rights movement.[14] As a final assessment, the students create "manifesto projects," statements in the form of essays, videos, or other visual media about an issue of their own choice related to the course. In the section of the course Chesnut taught recently, many students chose topics related to the damaging effects of gender stereotypes. For example, on the class's WordPress blog about body image and how it affects both women and men, one pair of students wrote: "Mental illnesses like anorexia and bulimia are developed . . . because of the need to have acceptance from society, to fit in, and feel 'perfect.'"

Chesnut has been careful to ensure that the course is skill-based and grounded in state and federal requirements such as those of the New York Board of Regents and Common Core curriculum frameworks. Yet despite the class's rigorous content, Chesnut says that in many ways, the "how" has ended up being as important as the "what": "In the way I taught the course, how I spoke to the students and encouraged them to take ownership, I think the trust that was built was just as important as the content I was teaching."

BIGGER MOVES TOWARD INCLUSIVE CURRICULUM

Teachers like Barber-Just and Chesnut, who proposed courses with LGBTQ content and proactively went to their department heads, administrators, or school boards with curriculum plans and syllabi, are rare exceptions in a school landscape in which silence about LGBTQ people and issues remains the norm. Leadership at the policy and district levels to mandate or simply encourage LGBTQ inclusion is even less common, yet there are signs that this circumstance may finally be starting to change.

In 2011, California became the first state in the nation to require public schools to teach about the contributions of LGBT Americans in state and US history under the FAIR (Fair, Accurate, Inclusive, Respectful) Education Act, which also covers the history of persons with disabilities. The Los Angeles Unified School District (LAUSD) then took the state law a step further by specifying that all LAUSD schools must address LGBTQ issues by:

- promoting positive images of LGBT individuals;
- making available age-appropriate LGBT-inclusive curriculum for elementary and secondary schools;
- requiring that newly adopted social studies materials include positive representations of LGBT people and people with disabilities;

- including LGBT sensitivity and outreach, education, and training for students, parents, and staff; and
- reminding staff of their duty to ensure that all students are safe and affirmed on campus, including, but not limited to, the prevention of LGBT-biased language and bullying.[15]

Directing educators to address LGBTQ issues has, of course, limited impact if these policies don't make their way into classrooms, a difficult situation to monitor in a district that encompasses roughly one thousand schools. The LAUSD has taken several measures that, while still not guaranteeing what goes on after the bell rings and teachers close their classroom doors, clarify the expectations at each grade level and increase the likelihood that students will receive an LGBTQ-inclusive education as the district policy intends.

First, the Office of Human Relations, Diversity, and Equity maintains an extensive website where faculty, staff, and administrators in the district (and, potentially, anyone) can obtain resources for addressing LGBTQ issues both with students and for professional development.[16] Documents on the site for school staff development include research briefs from the California Safe Schools Coalition, a state-level research and advocacy organization dedicated to improving school climates for LGBTQ youth and families. The briefs cover such topics as:

- "Understanding School Safety for Transgender Students";
- "School Safety and Students with LGBT Parents"; and
- "Understanding School Safety and the Intersections of Race, Ethnicity, and Sexual Orientation."

Taking the issue beyond safety, the site also includes curricular resources for teachers in the elementary, middle, and high school grades, some created by district staff, some by the California Safe Schools Coalition, some by GLSEN, and some from the *New York Times*' Learning Network. Lesson plans and other curricular materials range from those designed for use during commemorative events such as "No Name-Calling Week" and "LGBT History Month" (October); history lessons for teaching about the LGBTQ civil rights movement and related issues; a list of picture books for use with elementary students that address LGBTQ- and gender-related topics; and PSAs to use as a springboard for discussion with students or for professional development.

Websites that include resource links to LGBTQ-themed materials and even lesson plans are not unique to Los Angeles—other school districts such as Austin, Texas, as well as national organizations like GLSEN and the Human Rights Campaign's Welcoming Schools organization, also maintain them. But for LAUSD, having an easy-to-access website with resources already screened and chosen by district staff helps make the process of designing LGBTQ-inclusive curriculum easier and therefore, perhaps, more likely to be implemented.

Nanci Hanover, who teaches health at Kennedy High School in Granada Hills, California, says of the resources, "They are great to use as a jumping-off point," and she supplements the web resources with her own research and discussions of current events that relate to LGBTQ issues. (A recent topic in her class involved news reports on the torture and murder of gay men in the Islamic State.) Hanover also takes advantage of the district's prescreened speakers list and has had a speaker on "positive prevention" speak to students about ways to prevent the spread of HIV, an issue that has struck the LGBTQ community particularly hard.

"Whenever the opportunity comes up, I take every teachable moment," says Hanover. "It [inclusion of LGBTQ-related topics] isn't a standalone. That makes it look like it's something that's different. It should be part of everyday conversation." This is especially important, Hanover says, because so many students' lives are touched by LGBTQ issues: "When I ask in my classes if anybody *doesn't* know someone who's gay, only a handful of hands go up."

Inclusive History Books and Curriculum

As broad-based and accessible as the web resources are, they will soon serve as a supplement to another curricular initiative currently in development. In compliance with the FAIR Act, the LAUSD is in the process of designing a new LGBTQ-inclusive history curriculum in cooperation with the Los Angeles advocacy group Project SPIN (Suicide Prevention Intervention Now), the L.A. Gay and Lesbian Center, and the University of Southern California's ONE archives on LGBTQ history.

To supplement the new history curriculum, LAUSD's coordinator for human relations, diversity, and equity, Judy Chiasson, says that all future textbooks purchased for the district will be inclusive of LGBTQ individuals and history. Given the difficulty that even well-intentioned teachers have placing LGBTQ issues front and center in the curriculum, Chiasson says she believes inclusive textbooks will make a big difference: "If teachers have to go looking for it [LGBTQ-themed material], it's less likely they'll use it. But if it's right there in the textbook, they're going to do it."

EFFECTING CHANGE AT THE DISTRICT, SCHOOL, OR CLASSROOM LEVEL

Integrating LGBTQ issues into curriculum is easier to think and talk about in theoretical terms than it is to achieve in practice. Even progressive educators who wish to be inclusive of their LGBTQ students can fail to integrate these issues into curricula when the demands of test preparation, teacher accountability measures, and other pressures consume time they might otherwise spend finding and developing resources to achieve LGBTQ inclusion. Also, many educators just don't know where to begin.

These statements are not intended to exempt teachers of their responsibility to create and execute inclusive curricula; they are merely to acknowledge the reality that if materials, resources, and expectations are not made clear and accessible by building leaders, only the most diligent advocates for LGBTQ youth, like Barber-Just and Chesnut, are likely to follow through. It is therefore critical that school systems, as they do for many other curricular materials, make those related to LGBTQ issues readily available for teachers to use.

The Los Angeles Unified School District is moving toward this goal with its website of curriculum resources, as well as its soon-to-be-unveiled history curriculum and use of LGBTQ-inclusive textbooks.

Virtually all schools use textbooks in history and a wide range of other subjects, and what is or is not in these textbooks sends a clear message to students. Unfortunately, in the case of most classrooms, little seems to have changed since 2004, when a high school junior testifying at a hearing before the Massachusetts Commission on LGBTQ Youth said: "The gay rights movement is not even mentioned during the civil rights chapter in my American history textbook. I've yet to read a book in English class with anything more than the implication of homosexuality, and in all my classes when we talk about discrimination, we stay to issues between black and white communities . . . with all these people in my life ignoring an issue that is a significant part of me, it is easy to feel that I don't matter."[17]

When selecting new texts, school district purchasers like those in Los Angeles should screen them critically for LGBTQ inclusion or exclusion, and school leaders can work with department heads, librarians, and others to ensure that literature, videos, and other materials inclusive of LGBTQ identities are represented among the school's collections. Any school district or department with curriculum funds to spend can choose to allocate resources for the development of LGBTQ-inclusive curriculum, which can be shared among teachers within the department, an entire school, and even across schools. Moreover, web resources like those of the LAUSD, GLSEN, the Safe Schools Coalition, and other organizations are all available for any school staff to use for free.

As Chesnut's curriculum and the districtwide initiatives at LAUSD illustrate, history is a logical starting point for thinking about the possibilities for LGBTQ-inclusive curricula. Barber-Just's course shows how English language arts also provides natural opportunities through the choice of literature and writing assignments. But as education scholar Elizabeth Meyer has pointed out, there are also possible entry points in a variety of other subject areas. Meyer suggests:

- In biology, students can study the concept of homosexuality from biological, sociological, and historical perspectives and expand their thinking about the spectrum of sexuality by studying the Kinsey scale; consider the question of gender identity and the male/female binary; and learn in more nuanced ways about the hormones testosterone and estrogen, which Meyer says most biology books erroneously describe as exclusive to men and women, respectively.

- In fine and performing arts classes, students can perform monologues and plays that allow them to explore and discuss different gender roles as well as explore them using other artistic modes such as music and visual art.
- In health and sexual education classes, students can discuss sexual identity, orientation, and behavior in positive ways, beyond what she says is the frequent focus of these topics—in relation to HIV prevention.
- In interdisciplinary classes, students can complete research projects on social justice issues.[18]

Another researcher of LGBTQ issues in education, Cris Mayo, cites the notion of "critical and social justice math" as an opportunity to introduce LGBTQ and other identity-related issues in mathematics curricula. For example, students might learn about ratios to explore social divisions or the presence of in-groups and out-groups in a culture.[19]

Curriculum that is inclusive of LGBTQ identities can be a political hot button, as the proponents of California's FAIR Act and numerous other initiatives around the country have found out. The United States encompasses a wide political spectrum, from progressive college towns like Amherst, Massachusetts, to the eight states and numerous municipalities that include "no promo homo" laws on the books, which explicitly prohibit teachers from mentioning homosexuality or LGBTQ issues in a positive or even neutral light.[20] For educators who are seeking to make their curricula more LGBTQ inclusive, particularly in contexts where this might be politically challenging, it is especially critical to have clear, delineated policies in place that articulate the rights of lesbian, gay, bisexual, transgender, and queer students in their schools. And, as highlighted in chapter 8, generally agreed-upon school policies, core values, philosophies, and mission statements can help in making the case that an LGBTQ-inclusive curriculum is not only a good idea but is essential to fulfilling the mission of the school.

In the absence of district-level leadership, the initiative of teachers like Barber-Just and Chesnut makes a crucial difference in students' lives. As their efforts demonstrate, rigorous, skill-based curricula on LGBTQ-themed issues are possible and can be closely aligned with distribution requirements students need to graduate, Advanced Placement testing, state curriculum frameworks, and federal Common Core standards. Even in schools without an electives-based English curriculum like Amherst's, LGBTQ-themed literature can be incorporated into comprehensive English courses at any grade level. There is no reason, for example, why a student couldn't write an essay for an Advanced Placement exam on an LGBTQ-themed text. If that student is lesbian, gay, bisexual, transgender, queer, or questioning—or has LGBTQ parents, siblings, or friends—they might even excel when given the opportunity to write about something to which they are able to make a deep personal connection. And as the courses taught by both Barber-Just and Chesnut attest, a wide spectrum of students across all genders and sexual orientations benefit from engagement with LGBTQ-themed content.

CHAPTER 2

Transforming the Building

I N MANY WAYS, one might expect Jericho, in Long Island's Nassau County, to be a relatively hospitable place for the implementation of LGBTQ-supportive school programming. While it may lack the progressive history of Boston and its suburbs, Los Angeles, or the San Francisco Bay Area in terms of their widespread and long-standing support for LGBTQ youth issues, Jericho's proximity to New York City (it is about twelve miles from the city limits and twenty-five from midtown Manhattan) certainly lends itself to a community somewhat more attuned to these issues than many others. Yet where Jericho stands out as exemplary, even given its geographical advantages, is in the deep integration of LGBTQ issues not just at the high school level but also in the activities, curriculum, library, and even physical environment of Jericho Middle School.

Even in the New York City area, where many (but still not all) high schools have gay-straight alliances, participate in the National Day of Silence, and have other programming to address LGBTQ issues, programs at the middle school level remain rare and, where they do exist, relatively modest. When it comes to addressing LGBTQ issues, teachers and administrators often draw an imaginary line between middle and high school students, assuming either that the former are not mature enough to handle them or that their parents and guardians will object to eleven-, twelve-, and thirteen-year-olds discussing the Stonewall rebellion, transgender identity, and similar issues at school. So the fact that Jericho Middle School has had a large and active GSA (which now has about forty-five members in a school of roughly seven hundred) for more than ten years is exceptional. Yet this is just one way educators here have created an overall environment where LGBTQ issues seem like an important—and perfectly normal—aspect of school life for students, faculty, staff, and even parents.

PHYSICAL ENVIRONMENT

It is impossible to walk down the halls of Jericho Middle School without noticing the colorful "safe space" stickers on nearly every classroom door, on the door of the main office, on virtually all the office doors at central administration headquarters—essentially everywhere. The result of a design contest for students in grades six through twelve, the winning sticker (which looks professionally executed enough to be sold in any LGBTQ-themed store in the United States) was designed by a Jericho sixth grader and features a rainbow-colored triangle inside a circle of genderless, teenage-looking stick figures of various colors, along with the words: "Creating a safe space where every letter counts—Jericho Middle School and High School GSAs."

In addition to the award-winning stickers one sees everywhere, wall art, posters, and classroom displays throughout the halls proudly and unequivocally announce the LGBTQ-friendliness of this place, apparent to anyone who walks through the door. A family tree poster completed in Spanish for a class project and posted outside the teacher's classroom depicts a family with two moms. The walls are peppered with banners that students completed on National Coming Out Day. Students filled in their own responses to the prompts "I'm coming out for . . . ," "I'm coming out against . . . ," and "I'm an ally to . . ." Among the one hundred or so "coming-out flags" on the wall are handwritten proclamations such as "I'm coming out for . . . kids that get bullied" and "I'm coming out against . . . racism."

In addition to the hallways and lobby, other spaces at Jericho Middle School immediately send a message of LGBTQ-friendliness:

- The names of the school's Dignity for All Students Act (DASA) coordinators are prominently displayed in the main office waiting area, letting students know without asking where they can go if they have experienced bullying, harassment, or discrimination based on race, gender, sexual orientation, gender identity, and other identity categories covered under the New York State DASA law.

- The school library is a frequent site for LGBTQ-themed school events, such as a recent presentation and reading by Bill Konigsberg, author of the young adult novel *Openly Straight*. Whenever an LGBTQ-themed event (such as National Coming Out Day or the National Day of Silence) is held in the library or elsewhere in school, librarian Pat Minikel collects the library's LGBTQ-themed books, which are normally integrated into the regular collection according to the usual categories such as "realistic fiction" or "biography," and creates a special display.

  Minikel also works with English teachers and the GSA advisors to identify books and other materials for the middle school collection on LGBTQ-related themes. Entering the subject heading "LGBT" into the middle school library's online catalog yields thirty-seven hits, six of which deal specifically with transgender issues. The library of the high school, which is located in another part of the same building complex, houses an even more extensive collection of LGBTQ-themed materials, which middle school students may check out with parental permission.

- Through much of the year, the lobby's main showcase includes displays designed by the GSA to commemorate various events. For National Coming Out Day, the organization places several actual, four-walled closets in the lobby that visitors to the building can step in and out of to simulate the experience of being closeted, then coming out as lesbian, gay, bisexual, transgender, or queer. The closets are decorated to represent a home, a workplace, a school, and other places where LGBTQ people come out every day. As GSA advisor Elisa Waters explains: "We want to emphasize that coming out is a process, and that LGBT people don't come out all at once, but they have to come out to their families, their friends, their coworkers."

PROFESSIONAL DEVELOPMENT

The education of both students and faculty has been key to making LGBTQ issues a part of everyday life at Jericho Middle School (as well as the high school), and Waters has organized and facilitated both formal professional development and more informal, one-on-one coaching sessions with teachers about how to integrate LGBTQ issues into their lesson planning. Waters regularly teaches a fifteen-hour summer in-service course on LGBTQ issues in schools for district teachers, which she calls a sort of "LGBT 101" that covers such issues as LGBTQ identities, the risks faced by LGBTQ students (such as bullying and harassment), and the use of inclusive language. Although the course is not required, the district gives teachers professional development credits for taking it, and school administrators estimate that about 60 percent of district staff have taken the class. For teachers who wish to take their knowledge to the next level, Waters also offers a second fifteen-hour course on the curricular integration of LGBTQ issues in various subject areas as well as the district's SEED course, based on the national teacher training program Seeking Educational Equity and Diversity.[1]

For the last five years, Jericho has also hosted the LGBTeach Forum, a daylong conference organized by Waters where educators from all over the Northeast attend workshops, network, and discuss how to make their own schools more inclusive and supportive of LGBTQ students. For the first four years, the event was held in the school building until it expanded beyond capacity. About 250 educators attended the 2015 forum on the campus of the State University of New York at Old Westbury, which is across the road from the school. Although not an event specifically geared to students, leaders from the high school GSA are invited to attend, and Waters says it communicates to both the middle and high school students that LGBTQ issues are important and are discussed proudly and openly in their community: "They see this big conference going on here, all these people coming in from everywhere, and it sends a message."

NORMALIZING THE CONVERSATION WITH STUDENTS

Normalizing the open discussion of LGBTQ issues from the day students enter the middle school building is one of Waters' main goals in her work both with teachers and with students themselves. This begins with orientation sessions held with all sixth graders in their respective teams during the initial weeks of school. Coming from the relatively sheltered world of elementary school, students are often surprised by the openness with which LGBTQ issues are discussed at the middle school, but this early exposure to positive discussion—using words such as *lesbian, gay, queer, transgender,* and *bisexual*—prepares students for the way they will be expected to interact with one another as middle schoolers.

"We use real language with them," Waters says. "We talk about all the slurs—actually name them—and we talk about harassment, whether one actually is LGBT or is just perceived to be. They understand the concept of 'real or perceived' when they're in sixth grade." Starting this education at the very beginning of the students' middle school careers, Waters believes, helps them see LGBTQ issues not as a special topic but simply as an aspect of everyday life at the school: "We just tell them, 'Here, this is normal.'"

In addition to special events like the LGBTeach Forum and the GSA's sponsorship of speakers on such issues as coming out and transgender identity, the discussion of LGBTQ issues is also integrated into classroom curricula in a variety of ways. Beth Riccuiti, who has taught sixth-grade math and science for the last fifteen years at Jericho, has taken both of Waters' professional development classes and talks about LGBTQ-related topics both formally and informally in her classroom. In addition to math and science, Riccuiti coteaches a daily forty-minute interdisciplinary class with her students' humanities teacher that draws on school-wide topics being discussed all over the building. These can be related to the school's "theme of the month" or "quote of the day," which both encourage students to think beyond subject areas and discuss larger topics of interest to the school community, or to special events such as National Coming Out Day. (The "I'm coming out for/against" banners students designed were from projects they completed in the interdisciplinary class.) In addition, Riccuiti uses public service announcements and other materials during the interdisciplinary class to prompt discussions with students about issues such as bullying and respect for differences. She notes that having this less structured time to learn out of subject area constraints helps open up conversations that students can then carry into their subject-specific classes. But, she adds, it took students time to get used to them:

> At first kids were in shock at how openly we talked about it. "People are gay," and their jaws just dropped because they realize it's just part of our everyday, and it's going to be an expectation that they use it properly . . . But I've seen a difference over the years; kids aren't as shocked anymore. There's definitely still some giggling, but I relate it to myself. [I tell them] I would've been giggling, hiding under the table, when I was in sixth grade if we talked about these things. And I tell them how fortunate we are to be at a school where people are accepted for who they are.

Araceli Vidal, who teaches Spanish in grades six, seven, and eight, agrees that she has seen a major change over the eleven years she has been at Jericho not only in the way students respond to LGBTQ-themed conversations but in the whole school climate. Vidal incorporates conversations about LGBTQ identities in various ways, such as including a same-sex couple in a family tree she uses to teach the Spanish words for different family members, and in connection with LGBTQ-themed school events sponsored by the GSA. For example, on the National Day of Silence, a commemoration practiced in thousands of schools around the country in which students do not speak for the day to symbolize the silencing of LGBTQ people in society, Vidal and her students translated into Spanish the badge students wear to explain why they are not speaking in their classes. Also, on National Coming Out Day, students discussed the concept of coming out and related issues in a conversation that took place entirely in Spanish.

In 2010, Jericho Middle School also began offering a yearlong, credit-bearing class called "SEEDlings," a middle school–level version of the diversity-themed SEED class teachers take for professional development credit. Partly inspired by the district's rapidly changing demographics—it has gone from 95 percent white to nearly 50 percent Asian American in the last twenty years—the Seedlings class helps students understand and prepare for a world in which what they might think of as "difference" is actually the norm. In a 2013 *New York Times* article about the class, a thirteen-year-old student was quoted as saying, "I know thousands of things about every single person in this class. We're learning how to make the world a more connected place."[2]

Waters says these kinds of curricular integrations are simply part of what all educators want (or at least should want) for their students: "It's a cliché thing, but we always say to ourselves, 'Do my students see themselves in the curriculum?' You can't just have books that deal with race or those that are by and about women. You also have to include books that are by and about the LGBT community."

BUILDING LEADERSHIP

The LGBTQ-affirmative work throughout the Jericho school building—which houses both the middle and high school as well as administrative offices—is also part of the district's larger emphasis on social-emotional learning, according to principal Don Gately. In 2003, the district conducted an action research project and found that anti-LGBTQ harassment made up a major portion of the bullying that was going on at the school. Yet instead of simply adopting an antibullying policy, the district began offering teachers, administration, and school staff the in-service course that Waters now teaches. Like other educators in the building, Gately says Waters has been a significant contributor to his own education on LGBTQ issues and has advised him on how to talk to parents and other community members about the school's LGBTQ-positive work:

Personally, I didn't grow up with these issues; I guess I come from a classic working-class Irish Catholic background . . . But I would spend a lot of time with Elisa, talking things through with her, and we would talk about the kinds of questions we were pretty sure we might hear. I've had the occasional parent who has pushed back against this: "Kids are too young for this! They're too young to know about this!" I've gotten so much better at having these conversations than I think I ever was.

We've got flyers around advertising the GSA. There are no illustrations on those flyers. There's no "how-to" manual; it's about who you are attracted to, it's about who you want to spend your life with. It's about all the same things it is for heterosexual couples. But I have to say that all my conversations with Elisa and other of her colleagues have helped me understand it better. It's helped me advocate for it and make me a better leader as we move in this direction, to do this kind of work.

In the twelve or so years since Jericho has been addressing LGBTQ issues through professional development, curriculum, and other aspects of the school culture, Gately has taken the issue on as his own, becoming an advocate for the rights of all students. A frequent visitor to the middle school GSA, Gately says the need for a GSA at the middle school level became apparent to him immediately when, at a high school forum, students said how much harassment and bullying they had experienced in middle school. Now, Gately says, he is passionate about the need for LGBTQ issues to be represented in the middle school's GSA and beyond, a passion that is essential for effective leadership in this area: "I think it's not just about having the rhetoric at your disposal. Sometimes I think as a principal that's all you need. I don't have passion about the state's system for evaluating teachers, but I can speak intelligently about it. I think in this area, I think you have to internalize it. You have to believe in the cause of equal opportunities, equal rights, acceptance, celebration—you have to feel that."

The 2013 LGBTeach Forum, which was attended by more than 150 educators around the region, prompted Gately to write a post on his

regular principal's blog entitled "Why Our Middle School Has a GSA."
(See exhibit 2.1 in appendix A for the full text of the blog post.) Gately
says he is often asked by other administrators or by community members why his school has specific programs to meet the needs of LGBTQ
students when so many other students are also bullied and discriminated against. Despite all the work that has taken place in Jericho in the
last decade or so, he says much of the bullying he still sees (though he
notes it has declined dramatically) is still homophobic, and the need to
address these issues out in the open is clear: "One of the questions I get
is 'Why a gay-straight alliance? You have other groups that are discriminated against.' And the answer is, 'Well, let me see if I can get a club for
them, too.' Come by during the passing periods tomorrow. 'Fag, gay,'
those are still the pejoratives of choice."

Moreover, Gately believes that LGBTQ-positive programs such as the
GSA are especially essential at the middle school level because middle
schoolers are at an age when adolescents are at their most self-conscious
and self-critical. The GSA sends a message to all students, not just LGBTQ
students, that they can be accepted simply for who they are: "Middle
school kids are so uncomfortable in their own skin. Research says that
kids go through more changes between the ages of eleven and sixteen
than at any other stretch, except maybe birth to age four: intellectually,
emotionally, physically. They come to school thinking, 'I've got bad skin,
I suck, I can't get a girlfriend or a boyfriend, and I think I really should
just end it.' A GSA sends a strong signal to a kid that everyone is wel-
come, everyone has a place."

CONTEXTUAL FACTORS: DISTRICT LEADERSHIP AND PROGRESSIVE TRADITIONS

Certainly two factors that have facilitated the efforts of Gately, Waters, and
other faculty and staff to implement LGBTQ-positive programs and lessons have been the relatively progressive nature of the Jericho community
and a district leadership dedicated to similar values. The town's reputation for progressivism and its commitment to social-emotional learning
were a draw for superintendent Henry Grishman when he decided to

come to Jericho in 1995. Although in some respects Grishman said the community lived up to its progressive ideals, there were definitely limits against which he needed to push: "I did find that it [the commitment to addressing the needs of vulnerable groups of students] wasn't necessarily universal. While the seeds were here . . . there was some awareness around LGBT issues, we weren't doing all we could." Grishman says he then made a professional commitment to look closely at the school community in terms of "how we treat students in all regards." Thinking not just about LGBTQ students, but also the district's fast-growing populations of Asian American and Muslim students, Grishman believes questions of student identity are inextricable from a focus on academic success: "To my mind, this really isn't an issue of whether or not we teach AP physics. Why are you an educator? What should be our first and highest priority is to support and protect kids, and what does that mean to you?"

As a senior member of the New York State Council of School Superintendents, Grishman regularly facilitates roundtable discussions with new superintendents, those in the first, second, and third years of their work. An important aspect of these conversations, Grishman says, is helping new superintendents define their identities as administrators by considering how they prioritize among the many competing demands of their work: "What is your first priority? What is the single most important thing for you to do in impacting the school district? Is it the academic program or is it the culture of the place? Are you going to be measured as a superintendent based on test scores and test scores alone, or other measures of academic success—which is how we measure each other now?"

Grishman acknowledges that many superintendents in their first years on the job are unable to focus on anything other than test scores as a priority: "As a first-year superintendent, I can well understand in today's crazy world, it's not about kids, it's about test scores: Are you offering enough AP courses? Are kids getting fours and fives?" But ultimately, he says, focusing on the needs of individual students need not represent a diversion from academic success, and Jericho is an example of a community in which both of these priorities can work in tandem: "I think if you went into the community you would hear [about the school system], 'It's a place of academic excellence and it's also a place that takes care of my kids.'"

He also says, however, that not all superintendents or principals work in communities where LGBTQ-positive programming would receive the "minimal pushback" he has experienced in Jericho, and he has often counseled colleagues who deal with higher levels of opposition from school boards or community members. In these cases, Grishman recommends establishing networks of teachers, counselors, school psychologists, and others who can provide support for LGBTQ students in informal ways until more systemic change can take place. While less than an ideal solution, he says district-level administrators, regardless of their settings, have an obligation to attend to the needs of LGBTQ and other vulnerable students and make sure there are at least informal networks established to meet their needs: "It's your job to protect kids, isn't it? Do you miss some kids by doing it in an informal network? How do you not? But are you at least putting anything together informally where a group of five or six kids can meet with a teacher?"

MAINTAINING AND EXPANDING THE WORK

One aspect of the work at Jericho that both Gately and Waters say needs further development is outreach to parents. Although the district's LGBTQ-inclusive programs have, as Grishman says, resulted in "minimal pushback" from community members, Gately wonders whether they could be strengthened with further community buy-in: "I think we need to do more work in the community, more work with our parents. On a positive level, they know how much we celebrate and accept diversity . . . But maybe this is an area where ignorance is bliss; I'm not sure how much they know." Waters says one goal community workshops could achieve is helping parents and guardians develop the language to talk about LGBTQ issues accurately and effectively with their children: "We want to make sure those people aren't just saying, 'Hey, I'm OK with this' but [that] they understand the language. Give parents clues on how they can be better advocates. We haven't done a PTA [meeting] specifically on LGBT issues, and I think we should."

Finally, even when a school has achieved the level of LGBTQ integration apparent at Jericho, such an atmosphere needs to be maintained. Especially considering the influx of new people into any school building each year—new and transferring students as well as new teachers, coaches, and staff—the conversation needs to continue on an ongoing basis through faculty meetings, in-service classes, and other means. Waters says: "If things don't get talked about for a while, it gets kind of like a second language. We're kind of at the maintenance level now; we need to maintain the momentum. We need to maintain the energy. We need to keep this conversation going so as not to fall back into old ways."

LESSONS FROM JERICHO

"Safe space" or "safe zone" stickers on teachers' classroom doors send a powerful signal to students that LGBTQ topics are "on the table" in a teacher's classroom. Student after student profiled in interview-based research studies (including my own) has indicated that these visible symbols of LGBTQ-friendliness on the part of school adults make a tremendous difference to them. Even schools that are otherwise hostile climates for LGBTQ students can seem tolerable if young people have at least one adult they can go to if they need to discuss anything related to being lesbian, gay, bisexual, transgender, queer, or questioning.[3] Moreover, the GLSEN School Climate Survey has found associations between these safe space stickers and greater perceptions of school safety among LGBTQ students.[4] Yet, as I discuss in the introduction, the presence of a few safe space stickers among dozens of teachers' classroom doors raises questions about the climate of an entire school when only a few faculty members are willing to indicate that their classrooms are a "safe space."

At Jericho Middle School, the safe space stickers are on virtually every door in the building. Their collective impact is powerful and, in the case of this particular school, more than symbolic. The inclusion apparent in the library catalog, classroom discussions, afterschool events, hallway displays, professional development, and other aspects of school life communicates to students, parents, faculty, and staff that the entire building is more than a safe space for conversations about LGBTQ issues. They point to the presence at Jericho of what Peter Scales and Nancy Leffert, who draw on research with more than two million adolescents, call a "caring school climate," one of the forty key assets they have found that best promote positive youth development.[5]

The fact that all this is taking place in a middle school, at grade levels many adults claim are too young for students to learn about LGBTQ-related topics, is especially noteworthy. As GLSEN's School Climate Surveys have shown, middle school students are even more likely than high school students to hear homophobic and transphobic language in their schools on a regular basis, so it may be even more important in middle school than in high school for the negative messages students are hearing from peers to be countered by positive representations and adult-led discussions. Moreover, in the most recent GLSEN survey, only 7.5 percent of middle school students said they had access to a GSA.[6]

Clearly a central figure in making sure that LGBTQ issues are represented in positive ways across multiple aspects of the Jericho school culture is GSA coadvisor and Spanish teacher Elisa Waters. Waters helped found the middle school GSA, facilitates professional development on LGBTQ topics, organizes schoolwide events as well as the LGBTeach Forum that brings educators from other regional schools to Jericho, and consults with teachers one-on-one about incorporating LGBTQ topics into their instruction. Virtually every teacher or administrator at Jericho Middle or High School cited Waters as a key support in their own efforts to be LGBTQ-inclusive.

- **Sixth-grade science and math teacher Beth Riccuiti:** "A lot of what everyone knows here and the way things are here is because of Elisa . . . There's such awareness here. It just really changes how people are."
- **Middle school librarian Pat Minikel:** "She's [Elisa's] always doing something—she's the catalyst that brings so much awareness to the school."
- **Middle school principal Donald Gately:** "The best learning makes one a little uncomfortable. I didn't grow up with these issues. I spent a lot of time with Elisa."

In Jericho, LGBTQ issues seem to have been integrated into enough aspects of school life that many faculty members and administrators are now aware of the need to be inclusive and have the knowledge and tools to do so. But the role of a teacher like Waters at Jericho raises questions about both the potential and the limitations of having a key faculty person responsible for ensuring that LGBTQ issues are front and center in the everyday work of the school. Just as individual or small teams of faculty members often take responsibility in a school for issues ranging from curriculum alignment across grades to union compliance, having a point person or people responsible for LGBTQ issues seems essential when so many other concerns compete for the attention of teachers and administrators. As researcher Kelly Kennedy has noted, GSA advisors often perform this function in their schools, serving as a key source of information and support for students, parents, teachers, and administrators.[7] But teachers don't remain in their positions forever, so it's important that LGBTQ inclusion be integrated deeply enough into school culture that it can survive any staff changes.

In this vein, the role of leadership—both at the building and district level—seems crucial to Jericho's progress in this area. Both Principal Gately and Superintendent Grishman perform many of the functions Asaf Orr and Karen Komosa-Hawkins have identified as markers of effective leadership to ensure supportive environments for LGBTQ students: "encouraging and supporting teachers, counselors, and other school personnel to take proactive measures that foster positive educational environments; responding appropriately to complaints of harassment; permitting all students to express themselves in a respectful manner; and modeling the level of respect that is expected of members of the school community."[8] The school also benefits from being in a relatively progressive district. As Superintendent Grishman recommends, where systemic changes at the level of those taking place in Jericho might at first be difficult to implement because of community constraints, networks of teachers and school staff can help, at least partially, to fill these gaps and create the kind of "caring school climate" all students need.

CHAPTER 3

Turning Adversity into Activism

NOT ALL PLACES IN THE UNITED STATES are like Jericho, New York, where both the administration and community—as well as the overall political climate—are hospitable to LGBTQ-inclusive programming in schools. Discriminatory laws, powerful religious organizations with anti-LGBTQ doctrines and leadership, and political battles that pit progressive teachers and administrators against conservative school boards, community members, and politicians are a daily reality for many educators and their students. Such circumstances do not mean, however, that these educators cannot make a tremendous difference in the lives of their LGBTQ students and straight allies. As the teachers interviewed for this chapter illustrate, helping students cope with and develop the leadership skills to oppose oppressive political and religious forces is perhaps one of the most important functions a teacher can serve in the life of a young person growing up in a climate of anti-LGBTQ attitudes.

SUPPORT IN THE BIBLE BELT

Nixa High School, located in a town of about nineteen thousand people in southwest Missouri, is less than forty miles north of Branson, the entertainment destination often referred to as the "Vegas of the Bible Belt," and less than fifteen miles south of the national headquarters of the Assembly of God (AG) church in Springfield. Just six miles from the high school is an AG megachurch in Ozark, where thousands of parishioners gather each week and where church doctrine states that "God has declared great displeasure and opposition toward homosexual conduct."[1]

Spend any time in a classroom at Nixa High, and you get a clear sense of the religious conservatism that pervades this community, says Jackie Swindell, one of the high school's GSA advisors: "If you look around a classroom, you'll see students with bibles on their desks," she observes. And, Swindell says, religious beliefs against the rights of LGBTQ individuals are common among students: "That's how a lot of students feel in our community—that gays and lesbians don't exist or, if they do, they're going to hell."

It might seem surprising that a school so firmly situated in the Bible Belt could best all other entries and be honored with a national award from the Gay, Lesbian and Straight Education Network, but the gay-straight alliance at Nixa High School was named GLSEN's 2015 GSA of the Year. The group was honored in particular for the work its members have done to combat the anti-LGBTQ attitudes in their midst and to educate the school community—and even state and local politicians—about the need for inclusive schools and the rights of LGBTQ individuals in their state. As the school's outgoing GSA president said in her acceptance speech for the award, the honor confirmed the importance of the work the group was doing to combat homophobia and transphobia in a highly conservative community:

> I want to thank GLSEN for telling these students and our club as a whole that we are important. This is not a message we hear very often, being in the Bible Belt.
> When I first moved to Nixa, I was spit on, pushed around, and called names. In the beginning, students started a petition to try to stop our club. We stood firm and strong and are now one of the largest student organizations at our school.[2]

The current Nixa GSA started at students' request in 2013, just two years before the group won the GLSEN award, and quickly grew to a membership of around sixty, with bimonthly attendance at meetings averaging twenty to thirty. After a previous iteration of the GSA led by Swindell had fizzled in 2007, students approached Jeremy Charneco-Sullivan, an openly gay English teacher, and he agreed to coadvise the new group with Swindell. As Charneco-Sullivan explains, given the anti-LGBTQ attitudes in the community, one of his first priorities was to establish a "safe space" for LGBTQ students and their allies: "My first responsibility was to create a safe space, because that was lacking in our school community. I knew that the students needed a place to gather where they could talk about what it was like to be queer in such a conservative school and community. I knew that the kids needed to feel empowered and wanted to feel like they were being proactive as opposed to reactive in regards to their role in the school and community at large."

Charneco-Sullivan and Swindell knew that safe was not enough. Given the strong strain of religious conservatism in both the community and the school, they knew their students needed to feel a sense of agency, to take charge of their futures and speak out in an environment where many people around them seemed to want them to be silent. The GSA thus became a site for activism, both within the walls of the school and in the community. Students in the GSA mounted an antibullying campaign in the school and sponsored an "ally week" when they encouraged other students to sign a pledge not to participate in anti-LGBTQ bullying. Although participation among adults at the school was scant—Swindell says only a few teachers and no administrators signed the pledge— an estimated three hundred students signed on as allies, demonstrating how the GSA's message was beginning to catch on among the student population.

The GSA also took on charitable work in the community, providing gifts and food to families during the December holidays, and became involved with several political causes affecting both public school students and the LGBTQ community at large in Missouri. Visiting the state capitol in Jefferson City, they rallied for an enumerated bill at the state level to help protect public school students from bullying (one that specified categories of students protected, including LGBTQ students) and worked on phone banks to help secure legislation that would protect individuals in Missouri from employment discrimination based on sexual orientation (legislation that has yet to pass). As Charneco-Sullivan explains: "I wanted the students to realize that they can be active participants in the political process even though they couldn't legally vote.

To achieve this, we had trainings on how to lobby legislators. The students selected for the trip that attended the training went to Jefferson City on Equality Day and lobbied local representatives and senators about much-needed LGBTQ-friendly legislation. This included antidiscrimination legislation as well as an enumerated antibullying bill that would specifically protect LGBTQ students."

Two Controversies That Galvanized the GSA

Two controversies brought to a head the Nixa GSA's efforts to effect change within the school community. The first incident started with Charneco-Sullivan's request to use a chapter from the Zach Wahls book *My Two Moms: Lessons of Love, Strength, and What Makes a Family* for reading and discussion in one of his classes.[3] Charneco-Sullivan wanted to include the text, written by an Eagle Scout who was raised by two lesbian mothers in the Midwest and who later became an LGBTQ rights advocate and the president of Scouts for Equality, in a unit on courage and bravery. Charneco-Sullivan says that when the principal denied the request despite having approved all other readings for the unit, he appealed the decision to the superintendent, who also refused to grant his approval for the material. The refusals, however, galvanized the GSA and prompted the group to launch a campaign to bring Wahls to Nixa for an evening program, an educational discussion, and a reading of excerpts from the book.

"The community was outraged—people said we were supporting 'this gay speaker,'" Swindell recalls, while noting that Wahls is in fact heterosexual. But Charneco-Sullivan consulted with representatives from the ACLU and the local teacher union for support to ensure that the presentation would go forward. The turnout for Wahls' speech, which numbered close to three hundred, uncovered a core of support within a community where many assumed that sympathy for the GSA's mission didn't exist. Wahls focused his message on the need for students in communities like Nixa to know that they are not alone, whether they are LGBTQ themselves or, like him, are being raised by same-sex parents.

In a TV interview after the speech, Wahls, who grew up in a conservative town in Iowa, said, "When I was growing up in high school, it would have meant the world to me to hear from somebody who was in my situation."[4]

The second controversy involved Nixa's former representative to the state legislature, Republican Kevin Elmer. A posting on Elmer's Twitter feed showed a female member of the GSA wearing the group's T-shirt, which depicts three pairs of stick figures holding hands—two girls, a boy and girl, and two boys—to a book fair at one of the local elementary schools. The tweet read, "Nixa Schools failure. HS students working elementary school book fair in gay t-shirts." When an uproar arose over the message—and at the posting of a high school girl's image online—the tweet was quickly removed. The GSA advisors, however, took the moment as an educational opportunity. The following year, they arranged a meeting for GSA members with Representative Elmer at the statehouse in Jefferson City and lobbied him for support of the inclusive antibullying bill and a state nondiscrimination act protecting LGBTQ individuals. Elmer introduced the GSA members on the House floor, and though Elmer did not support the legislation, Swindell says the experience was an important teachable moment for her students. "We don't just take the kids [to the statehouse]. We educate them with statistics, knowing about businesses, so they can talk intelligently to our senators and representatives," she notes. "It's great for the kids to see that you matter. You can meet your state rep. They work for *you*."

The Effects of Anti-LGBTQ Messages on Two Teachers

Despite Nixa High School's national recognition and the small signs of progress in this conservative community, Charneco-Sullivan was one of two openly gay teachers at the school who ultimately chose to leave the district during the year Nixa won the GLSEN award. Charneco-Sullivan's main concern, he says, was that if he didn't move—he now teaches in the Springfield, Missouri, schools—his five-year-old daughter would be attending school in a district where her family wouldn't be affirmed:

I left the district because I didn't trust that my family would be affirmed and celebrated as much as the students coming from opposite-sex families. My daughter started kindergarten this year, and we wanted her in a district that would affirm her family to her and treat it as valid and worthy of praise as any other student's family . . .

The Nixa superintendent was very fond of telling people that the school was only doing what the law requires by allowing the [GSA] club to exist. This never sat well with me. I believe that schools, and people in general, should do what is right, not just what the law requires. All students deserve to be celebrated, not relegated to the shadows because the religious majority doesn't want to see them.

Swindell, who is a straight ally to the LGBTQ community, supports Charneco-Sullivan's decision and has begun to carry on the GSA with the help of the local GLSEN chapter in Springfield, a new coadvisor, and a growing cadre of faculty support. Their job will continue to be, she says, connecting students with resources in the area—such as the LGBTQ prom in Springfield and community-based student support groups— and countering any anti-LGBTQ messages students receive elsewhere in their school and community: "Anytime our kids feel defeated, they really feel supported by our group. We're really positive with the kids and make sure they know we're very much on their side."

WORKING AGAINST THE TIDE IN UTAH

In many respects that go beyond geography, Park City (Utah) High School, about thirty miles southeast of Salt Lake City, could not be more different from Nixa. Home to three major ski resorts and the Sundance Film Festival, upscale Park City is one of the fifty wealthiest towns in the United States by per capita income. A strain of artsy liberalism runs through the community during the film festival, and the school has steadily maintained a gay-straight alliance for the last eighteen years. Yet, like Nixa's GSA, Park City High School's group is an oasis of LGBTQ inclusion within a larger setting where forces of religious and political conservatism present special challenges. Meeting these challenges effectively contributed to Park City winning GLSEN's GSA of the Year award the year before Nixa, in 2014.

Located in one of the most politically conservative states in the country in which Mormonism is the predominant religion, Park City itself is about half Mormon, and state policies provide a less-than-supportive foundation for LGBTQ-related programming in schools. In addition to its highly contested recent battles about same-sex marriage and antidiscrimination protections for LGBTQ individuals (the latter of which has not yet been favorably resolved), Utah is one of eight states with what inclusive education advocates call "no promo homo" laws. These are laws that expressly forbid teachers and other staff from discussing LGBTQ issues in any positive way in schools, including in sex education.[5]

The Mormon church has a history of conservatism with regard to LGBTQ issues and provided much of the grassroots support toward initiatives in numerous states to ban same-sex marriage before the Supreme Court made it legal nationwide in 2015.[6] Given this larger context, Park City Principal Bob O'Connor has at times prepared himself for opposition to LGBTQ-related initiatives at the school, yet he says little has materialized: "I recognized the school's GLSEN award during the graduation ceremony, and I expected to hear some parental pushback, but it didn't happen. We changed the sign on the faculty restrooms to gender-neutral, and I thought there were going to be some concerned faculty members or certainly a negative voice from some parents. I expected it, but I didn't hear a single concern."

GSA advisor Mary Sue Purzycki explains that Park City's GSA has survived and thrived despite the prevailing political climate in Utah through effective messaging and the creative use of social media: "I think that what sets us apart is our focus on equality and safe spaces, and the fact that we use social media to spread the word of what we are doing." This does not mean, however, that the work going on in Park City is merely at the level of ensuring students' safety. In the last few years especially, the Park City GSA has risen to a level worthy of national recognition by cultivating student leadership and reaching out beyond their school and community to effect change statewide.

Fundraising During Sundance Prompts Activism

In 2012, the Park City GSA secured permission to sell refreshments outside one of the venues at the Sundance Film Festival, an event that for one week transforms the otherwise quiet ski town into an international meeting place for upward of sixty thousand filmmakers and aficionados. But what began as an effort to raise money for a small GSA led, somewhat serendipitously, to a major strand of the club's current work: involvement in some of the major LGBTQ rights issues affecting the state. In 2013, GSA members decided to use funds they had raised selling hot beverages during Sundance to the Alex Project, an organization dedicated to LGBTQ youth suicide prevention.[7] Then, in 2014, when a major battle for marriage equality was going on the week of the festival (the State of Utah had won the right to appeal a lower court ruling in support of marriage equality), the students' fundraising immediately became political. They decided to donate a portion of their proceeds to the fight for marriage equality and, playing to the progressive leanings of much of the Sundance audience, raised $3,300, over four times the previous year's total of $800, by telling festival-goers their purchases would help support marriage equality in the state.

Inspired by their somewhat unexpected involvement in one of the state's major political struggles, the week after the 2014 Sundance fundraiser the GSA met and unanimously voted to donate $1,000 of their earnings to the marriage equality organization Restore Our Humanity. Mark Lawrence, the organization's founder, and Derek Kitchen, one of the plaintiffs in the same-sex marriage case, came to Park City High to accept the check from the GSA. Lawrence and Kitchen spoke to students about the need for youth involvement in Utah, especially given the risks LGBTQ youth face in this conservative state. The GSA continued to be involved in the state marriage equality movement through attendance at rallies, town hall meetings, and fundraisers.

Social Media Campaign

In addition to the $1,000 donated to Restore Our Humanity, a portion of the proceeds from the highly successful 2014 Sundance fundraiser went toward expanding the group's social media presence. After Sundance, the group realized how much social media had helped their fundraising effort succeed. (For example, reporters and others live-tweeted about the GSA's fundraising for marriage equality, which brought more people to the refreshments table and higher receipts.)

The GSA established a Twitter account using the name @gsapc. Connecting almost immediately with organizations such as the ACLU of Utah, HRC (Human Rights Campaign) Utah, Restore Our Humanity, and GLSEN, the GSA Twitter feed linked to articles about the marriage equality case, information about local LGBTQ youth organizations, and other sources of information of potential interest to the LGBTQ student population throughout Utah. Between its Twitter account (which now has more than four hundred followers) and the GSA's Facebook page (with more than three hundred likes), the Park City GSA serves as a resource not only for its own membership but also for other students at the high school and for students elsewhere who may not have access to or may not feel safe participating in a GSA. As a description of the social media campaign on the GSA's website explains:

> The purpose of being on social networking was never to get thousands of followers and be best friends with celebrities. Rather, we wanted to reach as many students in our school district (and beyond) as we possibly could. We are very aware that there are closeted teens at the high school suffering in silence. In order to reach these individuals we created social media platforms . . . Because of the "no homo promo" law in the state of Utah, it can be difficult to promote our club. But, with the prominence of social media, we can reach hundreds of students and spread the message of equality . . . Members "live tweet" meetings, [and] we post the information of organizations like the Trevor Project and the It Gets Better Project, so our peers can have access to them.[8]

Future projects planned for the GSA include continued involvement toward the passage of SB 100, a legislative initiative to ban discrimination on the basis of sexual orientation and gender identity statewide. Openly gay state senator Jim Dabakis, sponsor of SB 100, has worked with the GSA, which plans to organize a community informational event about the antidiscrimination legislation. Other planned projects include:

- Assisting as servers at a local LGBTQ pride organization with an event called the "Prom You Never Had," intended for adult members of the LGBTQ community that may have missed out on taking a same-sex date to prom.
- Putting an international focus on the Day of Silence with T-shirts stating "Love Conquers Hate" in Russian, to highlight the silencing of Russia's LGBTQ population under the country's laws outlawing homosexual propaganda.

Working with the Religious Community in Utah

Principal O'Connor speculates that he has encountered relatively little opposition to the school's LGBTQ-positive programming because, despite its location in a highly conservative state and the strong local influence of the Mormon church, Park City is an enclave unlike most others in the area: "I have to believe that Park City is unique. We have people from all over the country moving here for the lifestyle that the environment and the ski resorts and culture provide for families. These life qualities have to attract a more open-minded type of individual that are choosing to live and raise families here."

Still, the presence of the Mormon church and Utah's conservative political climate loom large for students in Park City, even if they are living in one of the state's relatively progressive enclaves. Under Utah law, students must have signed parental permission forms to take part in the GSA. This means, as advisor Purzycki explains, that some students have to attend GSA meetings without officially being members: "We have official club members and students who drop in on meetings with no official affiliation." In addition, Purzycki says she has had numerous conversations with students who have had difficulty negotiating their Mormon identity with being LGBTQ, and in some cases tensions with parents have resulted in drastic responses: "I have had at least one student kicked out of their home and sent to 'reprogramming camp.'"

Several of the students in the Park City GSA speak to this dynamic in a public service announcement in which they discuss why the group is especially important to them as young people living in a religiously and politically conservative state:

- "In a conservative state like Utah, [the GSA] makes me see that there *is* support."
- "I am Mormon, and you need to be able to walk into an incredibly conservative church and you need to be able to find the good that's there, and find allies, and find people that stand with you, even when the rest of the community may not."
- "We are fighting the good fight here in Utah, and it's not always easy, but we're doing it."

BUILDING A POSITIVE SENSE OF SELF THROUGH LEADERSHIP

If the examples of the Nixa and Park City high schools demonstrate anything collectively, it is the importance of context in defining what it means to be a supportive educator to LGBTQ students and their allies. Two aspects of context that are clearly relevant to the settings of both Nixa and Park City are political conservatism and religion. In Park City, roughly half of the population is Mormon, and although this does not seem to dampen educators' willingness to address LGBTQ issues, the broader context of Mormonism and political conservatism in the state casts a wide shadow over how students experience what it means to grow up lesbian, gay, bisexual, transgender, queer, or questioning in Utah. In Nixa, the GSA serves as even more of an oasis than in Park City, not only within a conservative state and community but also—as Charneco-Sullivan and Swindell describe it—a school where not all students and adults are supportive of LGBTQ inclusion. At both schools, the GSA advisors have made a clear choice to go far beyond safety as a goal for their students, since helping young people develop a positive sense of self in the context of negative messages about their identities requires much more.

All individuals need to feel what psychologist Albert Bandura has called a sense of *self-efficacy*, the belief that their actions matter and can effect real change.[9] This need can be even more acute for LGBTQ youth and other adolescents who experience marginalization. Just as they are developing a sense of self and their own place in the world, young people from socially marginalized groups receive messages—in written or unwritten school curricula; in the laws that govern their schools, communities, and states; in the words of their peers and of the adults around them—that influence their emerging sense of who they are.[10]

In the laws of Utah and Missouri, in the doctrines of prevailing religions in these regions, and in the attitudes of many individuals in these areas, LGBTQ people are often more than ignored, they are vilified. Nixa GSA advisor Jackie Swindell recalls that the school received an anonymous letter after being named GSA of the Year and raising money so that she and Charneco-Sullivan could take two students to the GLSEN awards ceremony in New York: "It said we could sell our souls to the devil and go to New York or stay and devote our lives to Christ." To counter such messages, Swindell says it's important for her and her coadvisors to help students put such negative messages in perspective and realize their own efficacy, "This is what *you* can do to help yourself."

University of Arizona researcher Stephen T. Russell and his colleagues have highlighted the potential for GSAs to go beyond the mere provision of safety and support and to foster a sense of empowerment among LGBTQ youth. (Arizona also has a "no promo homo" law on its books.) Russell and his colleagues found that students who took on leadership roles through their high school GSAs felt empowered by their participation in these groups to effect change in school and government policies and to pass on a positive legacy to younger students in the school community.[11] In the case of Park City, students pass on the positive legacy not only to their younger counterparts but also to students in other schools who may not be fortunate enough to live in progressive communities that support a GSA. And this outreach even includes students in their own community who—for religious and other reasons—are prevented from being part of the club.

The role of social media in the Park City GSA is key, not only in its ability to reach out to students outside the group but also in the extent to which it allows Park City students to make a difference in the lives of others. Other schools across the country have used social media effectively in ways that allow students to amplify the reach of their messaging and make a positive difference well beyond the walls of their school. Blake High School in Silver Spring, Maryland—which won GLSEN's GSA of the Year award in 2012—spread its message of LGBTQ inclusion worldwide through a social media campaign involving its mascot, Allie the Ally. Allie is a flat paper doll in rainbow colors with whom GSA members, their friends, friends of friends, celebrities, and others have posed for photographs all over the world to show global support for LGBTQ rights and people.[12]

As I discuss in more detail in chapter 6, the need for young people to experience a sense of voice when there are forces that would silence them is essential to psychological resilience, the ability to weather the storms of negativity across multiple areas of life.[13] The educators in Nixa and Park City seem to have found ways to turn adversity into activism, to help students reframe negative messages into a motivation to effect change. As the Nixa GSA president articulated at the GLSEN Awards in New York: "When I first moved to Nixa, I was spit on, pushed around, and called names. In the beginning, students started a petition to try to stop our club. We stood firm and strong and are now one of the largest student organizations at our school. For those who have laughed, petitioned, or ignored us, I say, 'Thank you.' Without that, we wouldn't have been inspired to work harder, be louder, and stand stronger."[14]

CHAPTER 4

Tapping into Community Assets

ROUGHLY A THIRD OF ALL TEENAGERS in the United States live in zip codes classified by the US Census Bureau as concentrated poverty areas, where 40 percent or more of residents live below the poverty line, and well over half of all youth of color live in such high-poverty areas.[1] In cities, neighborhoods with high concentrations of poverty are often also characterized—sometimes accurately, sometimes unfairly—as being riddled with a host of other urban problems, such as drug trafficking, gang violence, and large, chaotic schools from which a large percentage of students drop out.[2]

This chapter profiles an urban school that, despite experiencing much of the stigma associated with being in a high-poverty neighborhood, has a dedicated staff that has successfully tapped into a wealth of community resources to create a better climate for LGBTQ students and their allies. The school has received two national awards in the last five years for its work, including the GLSEN GSA of the Year award for 2013. As is the case for GLSEN award winners Nixa and Park City profiled in the previous chapter, LGBTQ students at this school are learning to develop a positive sense of self in the face of considerable challenges that are unique to their community.

FARRINGTON HIGH SCHOOL

Farrington High School is located in Kalihi, an area of Honolulu with a reputation for being one of the poorest and most dangerous neighborhoods in the city. Approximately 70 percent of the students who attend

Farrington come from low-income families, many from the five public housing complexes located in the zone that feeds into the school. Despite its location in what is often seen by outsiders only as an island paradise, many locals associate the area surrounding Farrington with the same kinds of problems that plague low-income urban neighborhoods in other parts of the United States, such as gang violence, homelessness, and illegal drugs.

Ethnically, about 60 percent of the students at Farrington are Filipino, 11 percent are Samoan, 10 percent are native Hawaiian, and the rest are made up of various races and ethnicities, including growing populations of Marshallese and Micronesian students. Many students are either immigrants themselves or are the children of immigrants. The traditional values in many Asian and Pacific Islander cultures thus present another set of potential challenges to LGBTQ-positive school programming, so the educators at Farrington have included community outreach and communication as part of their efforts over the years. As longtime Farrington school social worker and GSA advisor Alison Colby explains:

> Despite these challenges and diversity, the overall climate around LGBT issues [at the school] is positive. Of course, there are quiet pockets of anti-LGBT sentiment amongst both students and adults, but because we have key supporters—administrators, the librarian, the digital media teacher, the student activities coordinator, counselors, other teachers—we have quite an accepting environment.
>
> Most everyone who gets to know the school and students is pleasantly surprised, given our reputation. I love the students here; they have spunk, resilience, and heart. And while they may have many struggles, the vast majority of them are appreciative, respectful, and inspiring to me.

Two Previous Attempts at Student Groups

Farrington principal Alfredo Carganilla says winning GLSEN's GSA of the Year award "was huge for our school," not only because of the neighborhood's reputation but also because the school has struggled to maintain the momentum of a GSA over the years. The current iteration of Farrington's GSA started in February 2011, but there have been previous starts and restarts of something akin to a gay-straight alliance since the 1990s.

In contrast to the usual situation whereby transgender issues are the last ones under the LGBTQ umbrella to be addressed in school programming, Farrington started with what it called its Chrysalis program in the late 1990s, which focused mostly on transgender students. When key students involved in that program graduated, it eventually disappeared due to lack of participation. Chrysalis was replaced several years later by a club called BLEST Gs (Bisexual, Lesbian, Exploring, Straight, Transgender, Gay Governors), which also disbanded after key students graduated. As Colby explains, along with attrition, another problem that plagued the two earlier organizations was the scarcity of funding common to urban schools serving low-income areas: "The other challenge we had with Chrysalis and BLEST Gs was financial. It takes money to run these programs—for supplies, transportation, and especially food and refreshments for meetings and other events. In the past, much of it came out of our [advisors'] personal bank accounts, and this became a challenge to sustain."

After the dissolution of the two previous groups, Colby and other educators who were passionate about their LGBTQ students' needs knew they needed to find other approaches that would be financially sustainable and would work with Farrington's specific student population of Asian/Pacific Islander and native Hawaiian youth, mostly from low-income families. The current group is run through the school's teen center, which also manages individual counseling, peer mediation, support groups, a gang violence prevention group, and other needs of the school's population. Colby believes the current GSA is more sustainable than the previous ones because of diverse community support and connections and the fact that it has an educational component with structured meetings. Also, Colby explains, adults guide the work, so Farrington students—many of whom face a host of other challenges in their lives—are not burdened with educating their peers or their teachers or with managing the logistics of GSA events, as might be the case in other schools' GSAs:

> We are not a club—we don't have officers or bylaws, and we don't depend on students to do the work. We know that for some, being LGBT is not the only issue for them, and we don't want to add to their life stresses by expecting them to devote all their time and energy to the GSA. In fact, we encourage them to expand their involvement in school, in addition to participating in and contributing to the GSA. The students come up with the ideas and suggestions, and we advisors do most of the organizing and planning—finding guest speakers; organizing field trips; researching, planning, and facilitating lessons and activities, with opportunities [for students] to contribute and lead as their time allows.

Graduate Students and Other Community Adults

To help ensure that the current GSA succeeded, Colby and her colleagues started collaborating in 2011 with a team of graduate students in social work and law from the University of Hawaii's flagship campus at Manoa. The partnership with the graduate students supplied the group with energetic young adults—several of whom were of Asian, Pacific Islander, or native Hawaiian descent—who could serve as role models and mentors for the students. These young adults also helped Colby and her coadvisor Gwen Murakami plan programs and add an educational component to the GSA. Even though most of the graduate students who had been part of this collaboration have completed their studies and are no longer affiliated with the school, the idea of lessons facilitated by adults in the community on various subjects of interest to LGBTQ youth has continued. In the past few years, topics for these lessons have included:

- LGBTQ terminology
- The Stonewall uprising
- Risks affecting transgender women

- Same-sex marriage in Hawaii
- HIV
- The role of allies
- Family diversity
- Harvey Milk
- Gays in the military

and even:

- Can animals be gay?

In addition to the graduate students, several other adult community members have donated their time on various initiatives in recent years to raise the profile of LGBTQ issues at Farrington. Josephine Chang, a retired attorney and now a consultant on LGBTQ youth issues, is a frequent visitor to GSA meetings. She has provided the group with books, videos, and other resources, and she has worked on various initiatives to raise awareness about LGBTQ issues around the school. She consulted with the school librarian on the purchase of resources from the American Library Association's "Rainbow Book List" and connects the GSA with a wide variety of support resources in the community.

"GOING LOUD!"

The GSA's biggest event in its first year of being reinstituted, one that energized and in a sense "rebooted" the previously dormant group, was also organized primarily by an adult community member outside the Farrington High School faculty. "Out in the Silence—Going Loud!" was spearheaded by Adam Chang (no relation to Josephine Chang), then a University of Hawaii law student who first became involved with the Farrington GSA through the graduate student collaboration and has continued to serve as a mentor and informal advisor ever since. The event was Farrington's response to a challenge by PBS documentarians Dean Hamer and Joe Wilson, whose film *Out in the Silence* depicts the bullying of a gay teen and his family's efforts to raise awareness about the need for accountability. Inspired by the work they saw young people doing in GSAs and community-based groups while traveling with the film, Hamer and Wilson encouraged groups to create events around screenings of the film and established a national award for youth activism, along with a $1,500 grand prize, for the best such event. Farrington won the national prize in 2011. In addition to the screening, which was followed by a discussion of the film, the Farrington event—which was attended by more than two hundred people—included:

- student slam poetry and testimonials;
- student musical performances;
- posters with quotations from the film displayed in the auditorium;
- an ethnic food fair;
- an art showcase featuring pieces created by middle school students and a mural by the Boys and Girls Club of Hawaii; and
- the unveiling of the school's new safe space posters.

Hamer and Wilson wrote a piece announcing the winners in the *Huffington Post* and said the FHS event underscored how anti-LGBTQ bullying experiences cut across differences of race, ethnicity, family income, and other factors:

Not only did "Going Loud!" organizers manage to bring together an incredible array of community sponsors and supporters to help amplify the event's message during two months of online and community outreach, promotion, and education, but they reinvigorated a dormant peer-to-peer support group at the high school and succeeded in involving local middle school students, the Boys and Girls Club of Hawaii, and members of a large, conservative, evangelical church. Perhaps most importantly, they used the film and their extraordinary voices and creativity to demonstrate that homophobic and transphobic bullying, harassment, and discrimination are experienced by, and must be addressed across, all ethnic, racial, class, gender, geographic, and religious groups.[3]

One of Adam Chang's and the other organizers' goals for the event was in fact to highlight the relevance of issues such as anti-LGBTQ harassment and bullying for young people of all races and ethnicities. As Chang explains, they particularly wanted to raise the visibility of LGBTQ Asian and Pacific Islander people and of the ways in which homophobia, racism, and other issues can intersect in the lives of LGBTQ youth of color:

> We wanted our event to stand out from other events in the country. For us, that meant making the character of the film (a white teenage boy in Pennsylvania) relatable to the predominantly Asian/Pacific Islander/Polynesian students of our school and our community at large. To achieve this, we needed to show that (a) homophobia was not just a gay white man's issue; (b) LGBT Asian and Pacific Islander people do exist; and that (c) race, ethnicity, class, religion, and sexual orientation all intersect.

To demonstrate how the issues raised in the film affected local students, youth shared their personal stories, the Farrington GSA students served as emcees for the event, and youth were invited to share poetry and music. Adult voices included Hawaii Supreme Court Justice Sabrina McKenna, who is openly gay and of Japanese descent; Filipino-Hawaiian comedian Augie T, who talked about having a gay son; and Principal Carganilla, who is Filipino-American and a graduate of the high school.

Managing the Intersections with Family

Coming out can be a difficult process for any young person, and the difficulties can be exacerbated when the child perceives that their parents will not accept the LGBTQ aspects of their identities because of cultural or religious values. Kylie, a recent graduate of Farrington, told me: "I would have to say that most of the Asian race finds it quite hard [when a young person comes out as LGBTQ] due to things like keeping the family name, culture, and most of the time children. I come from a Filipino and Japanese family, but I've basically been raised as a Filipino.

Filipinos are really strong with the religion and like to stick with tradition, making it quite difficult trying to bring up the topic of LGBTQ."[4]

Colby says she has had numerous conversations with students, and a few with parents, about negotiating family issues around a young person's self-identification as lesbian, gay, bisexual, transgender, queer, or questioning. Colby generally follows the lead of the student to determine whether such a conversation might be helpful or appropriate. She also notes that having an experienced parent advocate like Josephine Chang involved with her GSA (Chang has a gay son) can help in situations where it might be difficult for a teacher or GSA advisor to intervene but a student nonetheless needs help:

> We hope that our students know that we are here to help them if they want to broach these conversations with parents—but we trust their judgment as to whether our intervention will be helpful or not. Jo Chang, our great GSA friend and supporter for so many years, is a leading parent advocate and resource for parents in Hawaii. She attends many of our meetings and has gotten to know our students quite well, and they know that she is also available to reach out to their parents, too.
>
> When we do offer to talk to their parents, most of our students' responses are along the same lines: they say the situation will be made worse if we bring it up, and even if the present situation isn't perfect, it's not horrible. Once, I suggested to one of my students that he take home a video about parents coming to terms with their gay children. I thought he could play it at home, and it would possibly engage the parent in a discussion. But he said, "Oh no, that wouldn't work at all."
>
> I think culture plays a big role, too—respect for elders, for authority, for church doctrine, etc. And I believe that if we push it, there's potential to paint people into corners that make it difficult for them later, should their attitudes shift. I have seen support come gradually, and it's much easier for people later if they never publicly voiced anti-LGBT sentiment.

Keeping the Momentum Going

Another challenge the educators at Farrington face is that, as the past two attempts at a GSA demonstrate, maintaining momentum can be difficult given the ebb and flow of student involvement in afterschool activities. Maintaining this consistency can be especially challenging in urban schools serving low-income students, who often—in addition to schoolwork and afterschool activities—have responsibilities associated with work, babysitting, and other commitments. When a large cohort of highly involved students graduates, it can be difficult to keep the energy going, as Colby has learned is true at Farrington even after the GSA has won two national awards:

> It is natural for a large number to show up initially, and then drop out as the year progresses. We try to provide many opportunities for them to participate, but also to bond, so that they naturally want to spend time together.
>
> We have about forty students show up at our initial meeting, and then it drops off. About twelve students show up for our meetings every Friday, but they are not always the same twelve. I'd say about twenty are "regulars" whom we know pretty well. We make it a point to say that it is never too late to join us—we have had students become regulars after joining mid-year.

Colby and Murakami have kept the momentum going with activities such as "Rainbow Popcorn" film screenings, commemorations of national events such as the Day of Silence and No Name Calling Week, and field trips. (See exhibit 4.1 in appendix A for the GSA's 2014–2015 calendar of events.) Having been educated about the high rates of homelessness among LGBTQ youth, students in the GSA recently decided to engage in a community service project whereby they visited a runaway youth center, helped to clean and organize its food and clothing donations, and presented money they had raised for the organization. Several members of the Farrington GSA express what the group means to them by describing it as a sort of "home" within the school and the broader neighborhood:

- "It [the GSA] gives me another place to call home. It's important in Farrington, because it's a place people can call their safe haven and it's very welcoming. The people are kind, funny, and good friends. I feel like I've known them forever."
- "GSA is my second home. I always feel so accepted and loved. It is so important that everyone can have this opportunity."
- "GSA is my second home and family."

For a recent field trip, twenty-three Farrington students attended a reading and lecture at the University of Hawaii by nationally known transgender advocate Janet Mock, a 2001 graduate of Farrington High School who was active in the Chrysalis program, and author of the book *Redefining Realness*.[5] Mock, who is now based in New York, serves as a long-distance inspiration to Farrington students about what is possible for them after graduation, when they can boldly claim their identities even in the face of pressures to do otherwise. As one student who attended the Janet Mock event put it: "Meeting Janet Mock and going to her UH lecture was an amazing experience. Not only had she shown the students of Farrington that being from a low-income school doesn't mean you're not going to be successful, [but also that] *you* choose what becomes of your life."

THE GSA AS "HOME"

As stated in previous sections of this book—and as perhaps cannot be stated enough—gay-straight alliances are the centerpiece of work to make schools more supportive and inclusive of LGBTQ students. The benefits of GSAs have been well documented in numerous studies over the last decade or so. LGBTQ students in schools with GSAs are less likely to feel unsafe and more likely to believe they have adults at school they can trust and talk to about LGBTQ issues. Moreover, GSAs may have an effect on "straight" students as well: students in schools with GSAs are significantly less likely to hear homophobic language from their peers or to be harassed than those without access to GSAs.[6]

Although the exact number of GSAs or percentage of schools that have them is difficult to measure, GLSEN's registry counts more than four thousand such groups in the United States. In the latest GLSEN National School Climate Survey, roughly half of students responding said there was a GSA in their school.[7] GSAs are, for all intents and purposes, the law of the land. Under the federal Equal Access Act of 1984, originally passed to protect students' rights to form religious peer groups at school, no secondary school that receives federal funding may "deny equal access or a fair opportunity to, or discriminate against, any students who wish to conduct a meeting . . . on the basis of the religious, political, philosophical, or other content of the speech at such meetings."[8] Moreover, antidiscrimination laws in many states protect students and educators who wish to start GSAs from differential treatment on the basis of sex, sexual orientation, gender identity, or some combination of these depending on location.[9]

Like the schools and communities in which they are located, GSAs do not exist in a vacuum. As the examples of Nixa High School and Park City High School profiled earlier illustrate, the work of a gay-straight alliance can be most effective when it is geared specifically to the needs of the student population it serves and the larger community in which it is located. At Farrington, this means making sure that students understand that the LGBTQ issues depicted in the media—which often focus on the challenges and triumphs of middle- or upper-class white people—apply to them both in universal ways and in ways that are unique to their being from Asian, Pacific Islander, or native Hawaiian families. Particularly in the case of the "Going Loud!" event that won Farrington a national prize, organizers deliberately addressed what researchers and theorists have called *intersectionality*—that is, how various aspects of identity such as LGBTQ and racial identity interconnect—as it relates to students' specific identities as LGBTQ youth in Hawaii.[10]

At Farrington, Colby and her coadvisor Murakami also have chosen to involve more adults from outside the school community than might be common in most GSAs. Researchers have demonstrated that students in low-resourced urban schools can especially benefit from mentoring opportunities with nonparent adults.[11] And these adults can provide valuable human resources—such as planning events and school programs, as both Adam Chang and Josephine Chang have done at Farrington—in situations where other resources may be scarce. As Adam Chang exemplifies for Farrington, one advantage to high-density urban areas is that there may be an abundance of adults looking for opportunities to help LGBTQ youth have better school experiences. As he recalls:

> As a teen, I so very much craved to interact with other LGBT people. I craved it so much that I tried to join any and all LGBT youth programs San Francisco had to offer (there were only two groups that I could find back in 2002). Sometimes I found myself mixed in with the "wrong" crowd, and yet finding a place in which I felt like I belonged was crucial to me.
>
> I was twenty-four years old and in law school when I met with Alison at Farrington High School back in the 2010–2011 school year. I was working with various adult LGBT organizations in Honolulu to organize and plan monthly panels and events that addressed LGBT political issues. Yet there was a lack of youth presence in my work and on the island of Oʻahu. Upon learning that Farrington was looking for help in rebooting its GSA, I jumped at the opportunity.

In addition, community volunteers like Josephine Chang aid Colby and Murakami in their work helping families understand the LGBTQ issues that affect their children. In situations in which such volunteers are not immediately available, GSA advisors and other educators can contact organizations such as Parents, Families, and Friends of Lesbians and Gays (PFLAG), which has local chapters all over the United States, for guidance.[12]

The fact that Farrington serves a large percentage of students from families with relatively recent immigration backgrounds means that many students are raised with traditions about gender and sexuality that may differ from the LGBTQ-positive messages valued at school.[13]

As a result, some students in the Farrington GSA seem to view the organization as what psychologist Jennifer Pastor and others have called a sort of "home" space within the school community. In Pastor's and her colleagues' research with girls in urban schools, they found that having supportive spaces where students can "make homes" at school can be especially important for students who face difficult situations and/or need a place to talk about issues that are off limits with their families.[14]

Yet Colby's approach with families demonstrates a sensitivity to any differences between home and school cultures rather than a top-down imposition of her own agenda. Rather than pathologizing students, their families, and the neighborhood as being part of an "inner-city" culture that needs to be fixed, the educators at Farrington take an asset-based approach to their work, building on the strengths of the community with the help of key volunteers. In this and other regards, they provide much more than a safe learning environment. They help students feel affirmed and valued in ways that honor all aspects of their diverse identities.

CHAPTER 5

Respecting the "T" in LGBTQ

A MONG STUDENTS UNDER THE LGBTQ UMBRELLA, trans-
gender students are the subgroup that faces the greatest risks physically, psychologically, and academically at school. The GLSEN School
Climate Surveys have consistently shown that transgender students have
the highest rates of being verbally harassed and physically assaulted
in their schools, and they are the most likely to skip school or classes
because of fears related to their safety. The latest GLSEN survey found
that more than 40 percent of transgender students were prevented from
using their preferred names and/or pronouns at school, nearly 60 percent were required to use bathrooms inconsistent with their gender
identity, and nearly one-third had been prevented from wearing clothes
that conformed to their gender expression.[1] As GLSEN's data suggest,
some of this happened in schools that were ostensibly "safe" for LGBTQ
students: they had antibullying policies, gay-straight alliances, or both,
underscoring the extent to which transgender students are often the last
group under the LGBTQ umbrella to have their needs addressed adequately by educators.[2]

Even more than may be the case for sexual orientation, gender identity
is an area many teachers and school administrators feel inadequately prepared to address. In addition to being ill-equipped to incorporate issues
related to gender nonconformity into curriculum, educators may be fear-
ful of repercussions if they make what parents, community members,
and school boards might view as the wrong choices in their interactions
with transgender youth. For example, they might fear censure if they

use a name or pronoun in accordance with what a transgender student has requested, especially if that student has not come out to their family.

Many educators may be confused about what the term *transgender* even means, a circumstance that makes meeting the needs of these students all but impossible. Although definitions vary, the policy statement on transgender students of the Los Angeles Unified School District (LAUSD), cited in exhibit 5.1 in appendix A, defines a transgender person as: "A person whose gender identity differs from their gender assigned at birth, and whose gender expression consistently varies from stereotypical expectations and norms."

By most definitions, while many transgender students identify as the gender opposite the one they were assigned at birth (often referred to as female-to-male or male-to-female transgender youth), some might see themselves outside this traditional binary gender system altogether, perhaps somewhere on a gender continuum. Moreover, the word *transgender* does not refer only to people who have had or are planning to have a biological sex reassignment; for some, the transition is exclusively social and is expressed through dress, activity, and other ways that do not involve surgery or hormone replacement therapy.

Because so many educators are ill-equipped to meet the needs of transgender students—and because many teacher education programs fail to prepare candidates adequately in this area—schools need clear, explicit policies and guidelines that detail educators' responsibilities to their transgender students.[3] And, as with sexual orientation, issues related to gender identity and nonconformity must be out in the open in school discourse for any meaningful change to occur.

This chapter profiles efforts to meet the needs of transgender students at three levels: district policy, building-level leadership, and student-teacher interactions. Although our society clearly has far to go with regard to respect for transgender individuals—and the absence of pro-transgender school policies and practices is but one reflection of this reality—the work of these educators demonstrates how transgender students can not only be safe but can also be positively engaged and affirmed at school if teachers, administrators, and staff take deliberate steps to ensure that their needs are addressed.

A "GO-TO" PRINCIPAL ON TRANSGENDER ISSUES

Somewhat by accident, Deborah Smith has become a "go-to" principal of sorts in Los Angeles on the subject of transgender students. Smith's experience at the first L.A. high school she led, Independence Continuation High School (ICHS)—and in particular the desire of several students to attend school there as transgender—served as a catalyst not only for changes at ICHS but, to some extent, for the entire 640,000-student LAUSD. From the start, Smith—now in her second principalship in the system—was committed to doing whatever she could to respect her students' gender identities but discovered, in her efforts to honor their wishes, that there were "many layers" to the issue. "These students didn't just come to school saying, 'I want to use a gender-neutral bathroom.' They really wanted everything to change," Smith recalls.

According to Smith, several of her transgender students' attendance records upon entering ICHS showed that they had barely attended their previous schools. It wasn't until Smith investigated further that she realized that the students living as their identified genders at ICHS were listed by their birth names in their previous schools. In the absence of a clear districtwide policy on how to handle such situations, the attendance records were never cross-referenced. Since all permanent school records, such as progress and grade reports, transcripts, assessment data, and health and discipline records, must include students' legal names and genders—as recorded in government-issued ID documents such as birth certificates and passports that can be changed only by court order—Smith recalls that it took "a lot of advocacy" to clear up the many layers of confusion around the students' school records. "The confusion affected state tests, student IDs—it's not just about a bathroom," she says.

Since ICHS was a small continuation school, with five teachers and a population of mostly older students returning to high school after having left the system for various reasons, Smith says it was relatively manageable to work with her faculty to ensure that her transgender students' records were accurately maintained and that their gender identities were honored at school. In 2012, Smith became principal of Daniel Pearl Magnet High School (DPMHS), where a transgender student came out shortly after Smith arrived, followed by several others in subsequent years. Based on her experience at ICHS, Smith was better prepared to work with the much larger faculty at her new school to ensure that these transgender students' rights and identities were respected. She held meetings with faculty about transgender students' needs and brought in a transgender speaker for the faculty's professional development series.

Another change that had taken place between Smith's tenure at ICHS and her work at DPMHS was a revised LAUSD policy, which Smith had helped draft, that outlined the rights of transgender students in Los Angeles schools and the specific responsibilities that teachers, administrators, and staff had to uphold them. Los Angeles has had a policy on transgender students' rights on the books since 2005, but Smith was the only building-level person on a committee to make the policy more school- and classroom-ready, outlining specific scenarios and the responsibilities teachers, staff, and administrators had under them. "Who knows what this [the policy] is going to look like when it's out in schools?" was the question that Smith and the other committee members were charged with, she says. "I wanted the district to come out and say, 'These are the things you [school staff] will be held accountable for.'"

Before the new, clearer policy statement was in effect, Smith notes that faculty and staff expressed concerns about honoring transgender students' wishes: "[Faculty would ask] 'What if we use the student's preferred pronouns? Can we be in trouble with parents?' Now I make sure teachers know their responsibilities, what they must do. What are you held accountable for in the document?" (The revised LAUSD policy, as outlined in exhibit 5.1, requires educators to use the names and pronouns consistent with a student's "gender identity asserted at school.")

Along with her faculty, Smith also has found it important to work with her transgender students, both to know and advocate for their rights and to manage the emotions that can be stirred when students feel that teachers and staff members—accidentally or otherwise—are not honoring their gender identities. While Smith is very clear with her staff that willful disregard for students' preferred names and pronouns is a violation of district policy, she acknowledges that "slip-ups" may occur from time to time and tries to prepare students to handle them: "[I tell students] 'It's not unlikely that you will be called by your birth name. You've been here for three years. How are you going to handle that?' We practice that."

Smith's experiences also illustrate, however, that no two transgender students' situations are alike, and that faculty and staff must be sensitive to different family dynamics around transgender issues. For example, Smith has faced instances in which students were out as transgender at school but not at home: "When parents were involved [in conversations about these students], everyone had to backtrack. You can inadvertently out a child to parents. We had to be very careful that these students were protected."

DISTRICT POLICIES WITH CLEAR CLASSROOM IMPLICATIONS

On January 1, 2014, a new California law took effect to clarify the rights of transgender students in the state's public schools. Although state antidiscrimination laws already protected students on the basis of gender identity on some level, this new law embedded these protections into the state's education code, making the responsibilities of California educators to transgender students clearer and more explicit all over the state. School district- and building-level leaders now have the task of articulating to their teachers, administrators, and staff how transgender students' rights to attend school and participate in activities and facilities according to their gender identity are protected.

The LAUSD policies that Smith helped to revise served as a key catalyst for the changes in California education law on behalf of transgender students, and LAUSD's policies, in turn, were revised in 2014 to make specific reference to the new state education law. LAUSD's revised policy (exhibit 5.1) defines terms such as *transgender*, *gender identity*, *gender nonconforming*, and *transition*. It also spells out how district educators are expected to carry out not only the letter but the spirit of the law in day-to-day school practice:

- **Recognizing a student's self-assertion of gender identity.** As a general rule, school officials in the LAUSD are directed and expected to recognize a student's gender identity *as the student asserts it* and "as evidenced by an expressed desire to be consistently recognized by their gender identity." The asserted expression of identity, one that is consistent from day to day across every aspect of a child's school life, is key to the district policy, which states that "there is no medical or mental health diagnosis or treatment threshold that students must meet in order to have their gender identity recognized and respected" at school.

  The LAUSD policy makes a distinction between "official records" and "unofficial records" with regard to how transgender students' names and genders are documented. (Smith's circumstances with regard to her transgender students' records made clear, for example, the need to articulate how students' record keeping should be handled when they change their names, their genders, or both.) As noted earlier, the district is legally required to maintain permanent records such as progress and grade reports, transcripts, assessment data, and health and discipline records using students' legal names and genders, as recorded in government-issued ID documents such as birth certificates and passports (which can be changed only by court order). But in all other aspects of school life and in other documentation—such as class rosters, announcements, newspaper articles, school IDs, and yearbooks—educators are expected to honor a student's stated identity. In addition, students or their parents/guardians must be allowed to register in school under a name and gender that corresponds with their self-asserted gender identity without a court order.

- **Using students' preferred names and pronouns.** The policy thus applies to how teachers address students in classrooms every day. Educators are directed under the policy to address students using the names and pronouns corresponding to the gender identity they assert at school, and students cannot be required to obtain a court order, change their official records, or obtain parent or guardian permission to use a name in the classroom or elsewhere in school that differs from the one in their official school records. As a practical matter, the authors of the policy recognize that teachers may make mistakes when addressing a transgender student but state unequivocally: "While inadvertent slips or honest mistakes may occur, the intentional and persistent refusal to respect the student's gender identity is a violation of district policy."

- **Use of restrooms.** LAUSD school officials are required to allow students to use restrooms consistent with their asserted gender identity at school. So if separate facilities exist for boys and girls, a transgender student may use the restroom that corresponds to their asserted gender identity, and cannot be required to use one corresponding to the sex listed on their official school records. The district policy also states that, if any student desires increased privacy, administrators should make every effort to provide reasonable access to an alternative, single-stall restroom such as one in the health office, but that transgender students must not be *required* to use such facilities.

- **Use of locker rooms.** Similarly, students in the LAUSD have the right to use locker rooms that correspond to their gender identity asserted at school. Moreover, the policy states that if transgender students (or any others) desire extra privacy, school officials should attempt to provide accommodations, such as a locker in proximity to a coach's office or a "supportive peer group," a private area nearby or within the locker room, or a separate changing schedule.

- **Sports and physical education.** Although physical education classes in LAUSD schools typically are coeducational, in the event that these or any other classes are sex-segregated, transgender students have the right to participate according to their gender identity asserted at school. Similarly, opportunities to participate on athletic teams must be consistent with the student's asserted gender identity.

- **Dress code.** School dress codes must be gender-neutral, school officials cannot enforce specific clothing policies based on gender, and students have the right "to dress in accordance with their gender identity within the parameters of the dress code, as it relates to the school uniform or safety issues" (e.g., prohibiting attire that promotes drugs or violence, or is gang-affiliated).

- **School activities.** Transgender students may not be discriminated against and have the right to participate in ways consistent with their asserted gender identity in activities such as prom, homecoming, spirit days, and all other extracurricular activities.
- **School safety and antibullying.** School staff in the LAUSD are directed to "support students' rights to assert their gender identity and expression" and, as with all other students, take appropriate steps to respond to and prevent bullying and harassment of students based on their real or perceived gender identity.
- **Privacy and confidentiality.** Information about students' actual or perceived gender identities is shared only on a "need-to-know basis." The section of the policy on privacy and confidentiality also includes language affirming students' right to discuss and express their gender identity as they choose, and it reminds faculty and staff to protect students' confidentiality in cases where students might not be "out" as transgender to parents, guardians, or others.[4]

Arguments and Counterarguments

Policies like the ones in Los Angeles that specifically articulate transgender students' rights across multiple aspects of school life—including classrooms, athletics, and even locker rooms and restrooms—are highly controversial and have come under criticism both in California and nationally. Many critics of the statewide transgender students' rights law pejoratively referred to it on news programs and in public debates as the "coed bathroom bill."[5] Even some mainstream news outlets have focused on the "bathroom" aspects of the law while reporting on the controversy. (A headline on CNN.com about the California law said: "California Law Lets Transgender Students Pick Bathrooms, Teams to Join."[6]) Opponents have charged that this kind of policy gives students carte blanche to use restrooms alongside students of the opposite sex for questionable purposes, a charge that advocates say reflects a misunderstanding both of transgender identity and of how schools are being directed to implement the policy. Some conservative groups in California launched a veto referendum campaign to have the law removed from the books after it took effect, but organizers failed to secure enough signatures to get the measure on the November 2014 ballot.

Based on a local school climate survey conducted in 2011, the LAUSD estimates that roughly 0.5 percent of its student population, approximately 3,500 students, identifies as transgender. Over the ten years or so that the LAUSD transgender policies have been in effect, Judy Chiasson, the district's coordinator for equity and diversity initiatives, reports: "To my knowledge, no one has ever fraudulently identified themselves as transgender so they could sneak into the bathrooms. Never, I've never had that. Not once."

Chiasson adds that the explicitly articulated nature of LAUSD's policies regarding the rights of transgender students helps eliminate the possibility of their being abused and helps educate school staff about what transgender identity is. For one thing, she notes that the district defines transgender identity as the persistent, consistent, and insistent identity that a student presents, and students' or parents' requests to be protected under the school's transgender policies are handled by appropriate staff on a case-by-case basis. So students could not fraudulently use the policy as license to enter bathrooms and locker rooms, avoid gym class, or join an athletic team, as critics have charged. "A policy like this solves problems; it doesn't create them," Chiasson explains. "We've never had a situation of misconduct on the part of a transgender student [under the policy]."

In a recent interview with the online magazine *TransAdvocate*, Chiasson further articulated how the "persistent" and "consistent" definition the district uses to define transgender identity for school purposes helps to prevent the kinds of abuses that critics fear. And, she says, most opponents' fears about how students would abuse the policy are far-fetched and have never materialized:

The idea that there would be a boy who for some reason would pretend to be transgender, consistently present at school as a woman or as a girl—dress, attire, name, known by everyone in the school community as a girl—just to get permission to have the opportunity to engage in misconduct. First of all, it's ridiculous to think that a student would do that. Secondly, if a student was going to engage in misconduct, would they go through all that trouble to get permission first? People who seek to behave inappropriately don't go to authorities and say, "I'm going to be inappropriate. Can I have your permission to do so?"[7]

Finally, Chiasson points out that issues related to transgender identity at school are not just school issues. Rather, she says, dealing with transgender students' and adults' rights clearly and effectively at school helps prepare all students for the world they will encounter when they graduate: "Whether we realize it or not, we interact with transgender people regularly. Schools must prepare students to be productive citizens in an increasingly pluralistic society. We have to prepare our students for the future and not allow our fears to stand in the way of that goal."

SLOWER PROGRESS IN NEW YORK

In 2012, when a student named Lucas arrived at the Academy for Young Writers (AFYW), a small public middle/high school in the economically struggling East New York section of Brooklyn, Principal Courtney Wink-field admits that she and her staff felt unprepared. Lucas had previously been registered in school as a girl, but now Lucas had begun a social transition and identified as a boy, and he wanted to use the boys' bathroom at the school. Winkfield was immediately supportive of anything Lucas needed to succeed in school, but she wasn't sure how her staff would react, nor did she know what policies existed to protect Lucas's wishes in case opposition arose.

"We weren't prepared for how ill-prepared *we* were as adults to address the situation," Winkfield recalls. Working with ESL teacher and GSA advisor Michelle Eisenberg, Winkfield says her first step was to "see what was on the books" about the rights of transgender students in New York schools. "And we discovered there wasn't much of anything on the books," she notes. That same year, after years of legislative gridlock, New York State passed an amendment to the state's Dignity for All Students Act to protect lesbian, gay, bisexual, and transgender public school students from discrimination. Then, two years later in 2014, newly appointed New York City Schools Chancellor Carmen Farina issued a policy statement outlining the rights of transgender students in public schools. But before these policy changes, New York educators who wanted to meet the needs of their transgender students more effectively were left to figure things out largely on their own.

Winkfield and Eisenberg began to lay the groundwork first by talking to Lucas's family, once they had his approval to do so. "We knew that before we went to staff, we had to work with the individual student and the student's family," explains Winkfield. "We always start with the family when a student's not going to feel like their core identity when they come to school. So we met with Lucas's mom and talked with her, and we said our goal was celebrating Lucas and all his promise."

Although Lucas's mother expressed some concerns about his safety if he used the boys' bathroom, she supported the plan to help him live in school as a boy. As Lucas—who had just completed his junior year when I interviewed him for this book—explains, having the principal work with his mother made a tremendous difference in his being comfortable attending school as transgender:

> When I first came to AFYW, it was the whole bathroom policy, because I would use the unisex bathroom in the cafeteria, but not the girls' bathroom unless it was necessary, or the girls' locker room. And I told Courtney—I went to her, like, "Hey, I identify as transgender male. Can I use the boys' bathroom, because I don't feel comfortable with the girls' [bathroom]?" So we talked about it in a meeting.
>
> And then she called my mom, and my mom didn't know that I wanted to use the bathroom. And she was upset at first, because of safety concerns, again, but she was like, "Okay, if you're comfortable in school, then I will allow you to use the bathroom as a male. Just be cautious of what you do and, like, who you're with in general."
>
> So they [AFYW educators] take, like, baby steps with leading the parents, and like, "Hey, like how do you feel about this?" or "What are your thoughts on the topic of LGBTQ kids?" So they ease them into it slowly, depending on the parent interviews.

After their conversations with Lucas's family, Winkfield and Eisenberg completed an action plan, which involved establishing gender-neutral bathrooms and meeting with the ninth-grade team who would make up all of Lucas's teachers. Winkfield instructed them to use Lucas's male name, not his birth name as indicated on official school records. They role-played various scenarios and what teachers should do under different circumstances. In the absence of clear state- and citywide policies, Eisenberg recalls that some school staff were resistant at first: "We had people refusing to use the male pronouns because they had no training or knowledge [in working with transgender students]."

Perhaps the most important education at the Academy for Young Writers, however, has come from Lucas himself and from other LGBTQ students who have come out since the changes he requested have been implemented. "Lucas is well beyond his years and inspired a lot of students to come forth in terms of gender and sexuality," Eisenberg says.

One such student, Matthew, explains that seeing another transgender student who was out and well respected in school gave him the courage to honor his own gender identity when he first arrived at AFYW:

> If I went to a different school, I think it would like—I would just be depressed, because I wouldn't have the courage to come out . . . But then, like, staying in this school and then seeing Lucas coming out in this school, I'm just like, "Holy freakin' hell! There is a transgender student, and it's a guy! Oh, the world makes so much sense!" And, like, if I went to another school, I'm pretty sure, like, they wouldn't have an open transgender student or, like, a GSA club that is very understanding, and like staff who are just willing to learn about a student's personal history.

The GSA at AFYW has grown in the last several years to a membership of about twenty, and several middle school students have recently requested to join. Since the student population is about 70 percent black and 30 percent Latino, Eisenberg and other educators also engage students in conversations about what it means to be an LGBTQ person of color in American society. "We've talked about the issue, 'Is it harder to come out in the African American, Caribbean, or Latino community?'" says Eisenberg. "In the GSA, we encourage kids to think about that."

This openness around discussions of LGBTQ identity and race has encouraged not only transgender students but other students under the LGBTQ umbrella to feel comfortable with who they are and with expressing their identities in school. Tiffany, a student who identifies as bisexual, contrasts the climate at AFYW with that of two schools she attended previously:

> It's like before in my other schools . . . "There is nothing but Caucasians, and they're all straight." . . . And it's like, "Oh, since they're straight, I guess I should also be straight since they're straight. I should also dress like them because I go to that school." And it was hard for me to fit in, because I'm like, "I'm the only black person who is bisexual. But I've got to keep it on the down-low because I want to make friends." . . .
>
> And then I came here to this school, because it's like—you see people who are proud of who they are, and they aren't afraid to show it. And when you see people who accentuate who they are, it makes you want to feel proud of who *you* are, and it makes you want to tell someone.

Although curricular changes have moved more slowly than Winkfield would like, there are also signs of progress in this area. In their English classes, students now read Jacqueline Woodson's young adult novel *From the Notebooks of Melanin Sun*, the story of a black boy whose mother is in a lesbian relationship with a white woman.[8] In a recent project for advisory class, students examined "Coming Out in Popular Culture," researching the stories of numerous celebrities, including some people of color (such as NBA star Jason Collins) who have come out publicly as LGBTQ. Winkfield explains that now that the student body is more attuned to LGBTQ issues, many of the curricular changes come at their request: "Young people are now asking adults to have the conversations they want to have."

THE NEED FOR CLEAR, SPECIFIC POLICIES

The LAUSD policy statement on transgender students, which is included in its entirety in exhibit 5.1, serves as a model that other districts should strongly consider adopting (or at least adapting) for two reasons. First, it uses specific language not only to name the groups of students protected under it but also the settings and situations in which these students are most likely to be discriminated against or marginalized. This specificity allows school leaders such as principals or building-level point persons for diversity issues to discuss potential scenarios very clearly, what students' rights are under these various scenarios, and the responsibilities educators have to ensure that these rights are protected.

Just as GLSEN notes that enumerated antibullying policies help educators "feel more comfortable enforcing the policy," the specific articulation of situations in which transgender students' rights need to be safeguarded has the potential to help educators act in the interest of transgender students when they might otherwise be afraid to do so. For example, calling a student by a name other than the one on their official record or that their parents use might feel risky to a teacher to whom the expectation to do so has not been explicitly stated. The specifically articulated nature of the policy gives teachers both guidelines to follow and the freedom to follow them without fear of negative repercussions. Moreover, the specific articulation in the policy about what does and does not constitute transgender identity (such as LAUSD's language about "consistent" and "persistent" presentation of transgender identity at school) can help insulate a district from charges that the policy is merely a "coed bathroom rule" that students can opt in and out of at will.

The LAUSD policy on transgender students also helps educators navigate what, in many respects, has been the last frontier in terms of making schools LGBTQ-supportive. Even schools with active programs addressing the needs of LGBTQ students often fail to address the "T" adequately if at all, reflecting both societal discomfort with nontraditional expressions of gender and educators' lack of knowledge about how to talk about gender expression comfortably.[9] It is therefore critical for school leaders to address the issue of transgender students' rights and education directly if they are truly going to move their schools beyond generic notions of LGBTQ safety.

Some of the societal discomfort around discussing transgender issues in school stems from the notion that school-age children are too young to learn about nontraditional expressions of gender, or that young people who assert a transgender identity during their school years are merely going through a "phase" they will eventually outgrow. Yet the widely reported 2013 news story of a six-year-old transgender girl whose parents successfully sued her public schools in Colorado Springs for not allowing her to use the girls' restrooms illustrates how transgender issues can arise as early as elementary school. The Colorado Springs case also illustrates how parents play central roles—either as advocates or adversaries—in the lives of transgender young people. The educators at the Academy for Young Writers understand the central role that parents, if they are advocates for their transgender children, can play in helping schools negotiate workable action plans for their children's education.

For many transgender youth, however, parent relationships are highly problematic, and students are often out at school as transgender while being closeted at home.[10] Provisions to ensure confidentiality and not to require parental permission for a student to self-identify as transgender, like those at LAUSD, are therefore an essential component of any effective policy for the benefit of transgender students. More and more frequently, however, parents are also emerging as advocates for transgender rights, as in the Colorado Springs case and in the case study of Avon High School presented in chapter 8. Especially for children who identify as transgender at a young age, parents often are the ones working with school districts to ensure that the necessary conditions are in place. As Genny Beemyn, a scholar on transgender issues in schools, points out, we now live in a new age vis-à-vis transgender issues that allows educators to move their schools forward in unprecedented ways: "As transgender people achieve greater visibility in society and popular culture, more and more parents are becoming open to the possibility that their children might be transgender or gender-nonconforming and seeking to understand their children's needs, rather than forcing them to deny who they are. As a result, we are witnessing the first generation of trans kids who can actually be trans kids."[11] As the students at the Academy for Young Writers articulate, the efforts by educators to support transgender students—and the courage of transgender students to live openly—can have ripple effects that make a school more affirming not only for other transgender students, but also for students across the LGBTQ spectrum and the entire student population.

CHAPTER 6

Opening Up Spaces for Discussion

S TORY AFTER STORY of a young person's positive experience of school includes a special adult—a teacher, a counselor, a school nurse, an administrator, a staff member—whom they say helped them make it through. Relationships with nonparent adults, whether they involve academic support, guidance in planning the future, afterschool activities, or role modeling, have emerged again and again in studies with children and adolescents as a key factor in building their resilience against some of the toughest challenges they might face.[1] Students at risk or those who might be marginalized in their school settings seem especially to benefit from positive relationships with caring educators.[2] The GLSEN National School Climate Survey finds that teacher relationships play a significant role in the extent to which LGBTQ students feel safe in, engaged in, and connected to school. In the 2013 survey, students who could identify more than ten adults at school they believed were supportive of LGBTQ students were less than half as likely to report feeling unsafe at school than those who could identify no such staff members (36 percent versus 74 percent).[3]

One of the simplest and yet most powerful ways an educator can support a young person who is lesbian, gay, bisexual, transgender, queer, or questioning is just by listening. The challenges that educators can help LGBTQ youth navigate might include peer harassment and rejection, dating, and coming out, especially if they do not feel safe discussing these issues at home. As Jessie, a transgender student I interviewed for an earlier research project who experienced severe verbal abuse at home, explained, sometimes having just one adult in the school building who opens up the space for conversation can serve as a lifeline to an LGBTQ student: "Every school I have been to, there has always been one or two teachers I really trusted. Like, my drama teacher in high school was like that, and I knew I could always talk to her. So, I think there is usually—and I know this is probably for every kid—there is always that one teacher in high school or middle school that they felt they could open up to. I think that's kind of important. It makes you want to go to school."[4]

Research also has demonstrated that, in addition to having adults at school in whom they can confide, LGBTQ adolescents in particular benefit from having access to spaces in which they feel free to discuss their feelings and experiences *as LGBTQ youth*.[5] Gay-straight alliances serve this function in part (if not exclusively) in many schools and, as documented elsewhere in this book, serve as a lifeline in many school communities where they are the only space in which it is safe to discuss LGBTQ-related topics at all. But GSAs, by definition, are mixed spaces for students across categories of gender and sexuality. Beyond serving as discussion groups, they perform a variety of functions in many schools, including the planning and hosting of special events and, as in the case of Honolulu's Farrington High School, teaching students about LGBTQ-related history, current events, and topics—all in the context of meetings that might take place one hour per week. This chapter profiles three educators who, in addition to serving as GSA advisors, have opened up additional spaces in their schools for LGBTQ students to talk about the issues that are central to their lives.

GROUP COUNSELING FOR LGBTQ STUDENTS

Decatur High School is an urban school on the perimeter of Atlanta, a ten-minute ride on the city's MARTA mass transit system to the center of town. With approximately eleven hundred students, like many other schools profiled in this book, Decatur High is growing rapidly and gains between one hundred and two hundred students a year. A targeted Title I school, between 25 and 35 percent of students, depending on the year, receive free or reduced-price lunch. The racial makeup of the school population is approximately 35 percent African American, 5 percent multiracial, and 54 percent white according to recent figures, with the remainder being made up of Hispanic/Latino, Asian, and Native American students. Known for being a relatively progressive southern community, Decatur has an enumerated policy to protect students from harassment and bullying that includes sexual orientation and gender identity. The school has had a gay-straight alliance for more than five years, participates in the National Day of Silence and National Coming Out Day, has held faculty professional development sessions about incorporating LGBTQ issues into the curriculum, and has several out LGBTQ faculty and staff members, including head school counselor Ken Jackson.

A key staff member in charge of ensuring that Decatur High supports the needs of LGBTQ students, Jackson has been active not only at Decatur but also at the state and regional levels in helping to improve learning environments for LGBTQ youth in the South. He is one of the educators, community members, and youth advocates who steer the Georgia Safe Schools Coalition (GSSC). In addition to providing training and support for educators and families and aiding the development and maintenance of gay-straight alliances around the state, the GSSC organizes the Georgia GSA Youth Summit, maintains a resource website (which includes a hundred-page manual for school counselors on support for LGBTQ students), organizes student attendance at the Atlanta pride parade, and otherwise helps make schools and communities more supportive of LGBTQ youth. This wider reach beyond the walls of Decatur High is a necessary part of his work, Jackson says, because many students in the region attend schools that are far less supportive of LGBTQ students than Decatur: "We're coming from a relatively privileged standpoint [relative to other schools in the South]."

In addition to being a cosponsor of the school's GSA and chaperoning the community LGBTQ prom, which also includes students from neighboring schools, Jackson facilitates a weekly counseling group specifically for LGBTQ-identified students. Unlike the gay-straight alliance—in which students can participate across all sexual orientations and gender identities—the counseling group is specifically for students who identify somewhere on the LGBTQ spectrum. As Jackson clarifies, however, this might encompass any of the following: "lesbian, gay, bisexual, transgender, queer, questioning, unsure, or 'to be announced.'"

Jackson's is one of several counseling groups in which Decatur students may choose to participate. The sessions are organized during rotating class periods so that students don't miss a particular class more than once a month, and students are given a needs survey at the beginning of the year to determine what counseling groups might interest them. Since all students are required to turn in these surveys (which the school calls *advisory sheets*), potential members of the LGBTQ support group don't need to self-identify in front of their peers or, at first, even to the counselors. As school librarian and advisor Laura Nolan explains, "[In the advisories] every kid feels like there's someone else like them at the school."

Without "outing" students or asking them direct questions about their sexual orientation or gender identity, Jackson and the other counselors follow up the advisory sheet with a prescreening form (see exhibit 6.1 in appendix A) and conversation to determine if a counseling group, such as the LGBTQ gathering, might be beneficial for a student. Students who decide they want to join the counseling group can participate for as long as they wish. They are generally asked to commit to it for six months, but they are then free to come and go on an "as needed" basis. For this reason, participation in what the students frequently refer to in shorthand as "group" ranges from roughly eight members to as many as twenty, and either one or two groups meet per week at any given time based on the number of students involved.

Jackson notes that just as a GSA is an important resource for all students, LGBTQ and straight, having counseling sessions where students all identify as LGBTQ has its own benefits. Given the rejection they can face from peers, family members, and religious communities, Jackson says LGBTQ students can be especially vulnerable to anxiety, stress, and depression. With clear, agreed-upon rules about confidentiality, Jackson says the group discusses challenges specific to being LGBTQ, such as coming out or dating, and sometimes they just talk about "other stuff," such as problems in their families or academics. As Shelby, a recent graduate of Decatur High School who participated in Jackson's counseling group, reports, both the group and Jackson as a counselor helped her navigate the challenges she experienced from academic pressures as well as the stresses associated with coming out as bisexual:

> I began questioning my sexuality at the end of eighth grade and began figuring things out my freshman year of high school. A friend of mine at the time, who was also my first girl crush, encouraged me to sign up for the LGBTQ group my first week of high school, so I did it. For my freshman year, it helped me figure out my sexuality in a safe environment and talk about my questioning in a place where people wouldn't judge me. It's hard to tell people "I may or may not like girls." People don't believe you unless you have a more definite answer. Even as a bisexual, people don't believe you as much as they would someone who says they're gay. So it was nice to figure that out in a group where other people were going through the same thing.
>
> Even after I settled upon my sexuality—I like boys, I like girls, therefore I label myself as bisexual—it was immensely helpful to have a place I could talk about my problems once a week. Group was helpful because everyone had a different perspective and could help me think of things differently. As I experienced depression my sophomore and junior year, talking about those dark feelings was a blessing, especially because others in the group knew what I was talking about. A lot of LGBTQ youth suffer from depression, so I knew I wasn't alone.
>
> In group, I could voice thoughts like "I think I'm about to date this beautiful friend of mine" and "I think I'm going to come out to my parents for this girl so I won't be sneaking around." Sometimes, being LGBT was only a uniting factor in the group when we had to sort things out in our life. After I had figured out my sexuality, I sometimes felt like being in group helped me more with depression and stress than it did with problems with my sexuality. Being from Decatur, I never really found someone who openly hated me for being bi. Still, that common factor made it easier to relate to others.

I often said that I don't know how I would have gotten through high school without a few things—sad girl music, writing, and of course, group. Dr. Jackson became someone I could confide in even with things irrelevant to LGBT struggles, like college rejection, parental pressure, intense stress, and loneliness.[6]

As a school counselor, Jackson is also well equipped to assist students in the LGBTQ support group with ideas and resources for planning college and other aspects of their futures. "For example, we've had conversations about how to find an LGBT-friendly college," he says. And the fact that Jackson is out to students as gay (with a picture of him and his husband in his office serving as a visual reminder) seems to help students feel as though they can talk about anything related to being LGBTQ in the space of the counseling sessions. As Jackson explained recently in an article for the publication *School Counselor*: "I strongly believe that LGBTQ students need role models like themselves. When I was in a very oppressive place and had no voice to talk about these issues, a faculty member said to me, 'At least every day they can see you in the classroom and that makes a difference, just knowing there is someone like them and they are not alone.' "[7]

Even though students miss a section of one of their classes each month to attend the counseling sessions, Jackson says most faculty support the idea because they recognize the link between social and emotional well-being and academic performance: "We make the case that if you attend to students' emotional and mental health, they make better grades in your classroom."

BOOK DISCUSSION GROUPS: FINDING A VOICE THROUGH LITERATURE

Betty Herzhauser teaches English and is the department cochair at Osceola High School in Seminole, Florida, located in the western part of the state between Tampa and St. Petersburg. Though a trusted ally to LGBTQ students for many years, Herzhauser's specific work on LGBTQ issues at the school began in 2009, first as the founding advisor of a gay-straight alliance, then as the facilitator of a book club that frequently reads and discusses LGBTQ-themed titles.

Herzhauser says one of the reasons she believes that students chose her as a potential faculty advisor of the GSA was the openness to LGBTQ issues that was already apparent in her classroom: "Students are free to research LGBT authors or issues for research papers. I have GLSEN safe space posters and stickers on my door. I discuss the effects of bullying on students. I include literature by and about LGBT individuals in my classroom."

Herzhauser also believes she was nominated as GSA advisor because one of the students who wanted to initiate the club had recently come out to her as gay in a paper he wrote for her English class. She says the student (David, a pseudonym) was pleasantly surprised by her some-what blasé reaction, since she didn't express any concerns or ask any follow-up questions about it: "I told him he was still just David to me. He had just added a new piece of information."

As is common when gay-straight alliances are initiated in schools that have not had them before, posters announcing the GSA's first meetings were torn down in the early days of the organization, but the protest was short-lived. Given the strong conservative Christian presence in this Florida community, Herzhauser reports there also was some initial tension when members of the Christian student group objected to the school's participation in the National Day of Silence and argued for their own day of silence to draw attention to the ways Christians are persecuted around the world. Initially a dispute that seemed to pit the two groups against each other, the controversy ultimately resulted in an opportunity for both student groups to recognize each other's points of view and find some common ground: "We had a good discussion about the rights of people and how to stand in solidarity with people we may or may not agree with. By the same token, I had discussions with the GSA students about appreciating the strong faith of their classmates and the courage it takes to stand up for their beliefs. We have had no real issues since."

Overall, the climate at Osceola seems to have moved toward greater openness about LGBTQ issues in recent years. A few years ago, a trans-gender boy was elected by his peers as a member of the prom court (though he was not elected king), and participation in the National Day of Silence has grown to about seventy-five students. GSA membership stands at around thirty (with weekly meeting attendance hovering around twenty, according to Herzhauser) and students are already looking to change the name of the GSA in order to make it more inclusive. A recent proposal by students would rename the organization SAGE (Sexuality and Gender Equality) to recognize the wide spectrum of sexual and gender identities that exists both in the school and in society.

The idea for a book discussion group came quickly on the heels of the GSA and was also student-inspired. The book club does not officially have an LGBTQ focus, but LGBTQ titles are frequent choices with the group because many of the club participants are also GSA members. Herzhauser already had several LGBTQ-themed pieces of literature in her classroom library, which included titles such as *Ash* by Malinda Lo, a retelling of the Cinderella fairy tale with a lesbian love story at the center, and *Boy Meets Boy* by David Levithan, which depicts an imaginary high school where LGBTQ students are at the top of the social hierarchy.[8] The Levithan book, Herzhauser recalls, provoked a lively discussion as students considered what a school culture free of homophobia might look like: "I remember when we were discussing *Boy Meets Boy*. The kids were saying, 'But people won't ever be this nice!' And I encouraged them to think about, 'Yeah, but what if they were? What would it take to make that happen?'"

Supplementing books she already had on the shelf, Herzhauser then worked with the students to come up with a more comprehensive list from which they could choose titles for the club to discuss. She drew on topics that seemed to come up frequently in discussions among GSA members, such as transgender youths' transitioning, bullying, and LGBTQ rights; materials she learned about at national conferences, such as that of the National Council of Teachers of English (NCTE); and winners of LGBTQ book prizes, such as the Lambda Literary Awards: "They [students] were genuinely surprised by the number of titles, and they quickly checked out several from my shelves and learned how many were available in our school's library. Through interlibrary loan, we have been able to secure copies of titles for group discussion. Discussions just follow organically after they have read books because they open up the topic and make it accessible." To take the book discussions to the next level, the group now plans to work with the library media specialist on making titles on its discussion list available in electronic form, so that they can have easy access to them on their laptops, tablets, and smartphones.

Teachers of literature often explain its value in terms of "windows and mirrors," opportunities for students both to look out into worlds different from their own ("windows") and to see their own experiences reflected through the "mirrors" of books about people who share similar experiences.[9] Herzhauser says reading and discussing LGBTQ-themed literature helps all students in the book group gain a window into a life different from their own and, for the LGBTQ participants, a way to look toward the future with optimism: "The use of LGBTQ texts gives young adults the opportunity to see themselves in literature or to observe people they may know or want to be through a fictional or nonfictional account. It is not unusual for young adults to find hope in a book."

ONE-ON-ONE MENTORING: THE STUDENT-TEACHER RELATIONSHIP

Creating organized spaces such as counseling groups or book clubs is a way for teachers to encourage dialogue among students about the issues associated with being LGBTQ that might complement or extend conversations taking place in the GSA. Another way is simply to be, as Jessie says at the beginning of this chapter, "that one teacher" students know they can trust with concerns that they don't feel comfortable talking about at home or elsewhere at school.

Nearly twenty years ago, a student went to a faculty meeting at Taft High School in Los Angeles and asked if any teachers would be willing to sponsor a gay-straight alliance (known as Project 10 in most Los Angeles schools). Teacher Bridget Brownell recalls asking, "I'm straight. Can I do it?" Brownell says she has since watched the GSA grow from a quiet group of five or so students to a proud membership approaching fifty youth. She also has worked with the school librarian to expand the school's collection of LGBTQ-themed titles and has participated with her students in countless citywide events to celebrate LGBTQ pride.

A health education teacher, Brownell has at times struggled with cost-cutting attempts at the state and city level that threaten her curriculum, but she says it is particularly important for LGBTQ students and offers numerous opportunities to discuss important issues in their lives. For example, she has brought in speakers from the Trevor Project, an organization dedicated to preventing LGBTQ youth suicide: "I know that my subject lends itself to teaching how to stand up for others (in the communications unit) and for talking about LGBTQIA relationships.[10] We spend five days on the subject as part of the human sexuality unit, [and] have guest speakers from GLIDE [Gays and Lesbians Initiating a Dialogue for Equality] and/or the Trevor Project. We review terminology and myths . . . we read the first story in [the LGBTQ-themed young adult anthology] *Am I Blue*."[11]

Over the years, Brownell has counseled many LGBTQ students on issues from coming out to dealing with substance abuse (a risk to which LGBTQ youth are particularly vulnerable).[12] In at least a few cases, the trust she has built with students has had a lasting effect into their adulthood, as evidenced by two former students of Brownell's who contacted me via e-mail for this project.

Melissa: I went to Taft High School from 1996 through 2000, during which time Bridget Brownell was involved in starting the Project 10 LGBTQ club. The general culture at Taft during that time lacked today's value placed on individuality and anti-bullying. It was never violent, however some verbal harassment and many dirty looks were a part of my daily life as a female with extremely short hair and clothing that strayed from the norm. I was forced to develop defense mechanisms and coping skills to deal with the daily anxiety and pain of being so uncomfortable in the environment I had to spend so much of my youth in. I was overjoyed when the first club meeting finally arrived. It was a relief to have a club that provided a safe place and way to connect with new people.

In addition to her involvement with the LGBTQ club, it was widely known that Ms. Brownell always made herself available to students who needed her. Recently I had dinner with an old friend who was a student at Taft, but never in Ms. Brownell's class. They told me that Ms. Brownell had helped them leave their abusive home and enter the foster system. Even though they had never met, my friend knew they should go to Ms. Brownell. She was the only teacher who had such a reputation for kindness and compassion.

By my senior year I had previously been in Ms. Brownell's class and been involved in the LGBTQ club, so I had signed up to be her teaching assistant. I had confided in her many times and we had developed a great rapport. I had started using hard drugs at 14, and by my senior year I was using every day. I was experiencing effects of addiction, and Ms. Brownell had expressed to me that she was worried. I tried to slow down, but she eventually told me that I needed to tell my parents, or she and I could tell them together.

So we invited my mom for a parent-teacher conference after school, and we told her that I was having trouble and needed help. My mother was shocked, but extremely supportive, and she told me that she just thought I was going to come out. So, I took that conversation topic as an opportunity to do so. After Ms. Brownell pushed me to talk to my parents, I struggled to get sober with their help, and eventually successfully did so after graduation. By her stepping in and having me tell my parents, I was able to get the support and help I needed to finally change my life. If I had continued using drugs, my life would have been horribly different today or over. I am so grateful to Ms. Brownell for pushing me in the right direction and helping me have the conversation that started changing my life, and truly saved my life. Currently I have 14 years clean and sober. I live with my fantastically sweet and smart girlfriend, our two cats, and new dog.

Victor: As an LGBT alumni of Taft High School, I must thank my senior year health and life skills teacher, Ms. Brownell, for creating a welcoming and understanding environment for all students. I was closeted for the majority of my high school career (2008–2012) and only began to come out to my inner circle in the middle of my senior year, due in large part to her vocal acceptance of students who identified as LGBTQ.

As a largely closeted student, Taft's GSA didn't appeal to me. Although it was described as a "gay-straight alliance," there was rarely ever a straight student involved in the club. Had I joined, I would've immediately outed myself. I wasn't prepared for that mentally or emotionally . . .

However, progressing through high school, I became more and more aware of the love and support students were offered by their teachers in an individual setting . . . If it weren't for teachers like Ms. Brownell and countless others, I don't think I would've been comfortable enough to come out at the time that I did. While I wish I had the capacity to do so earlier like many LGBTQ youth do now, I am certain that my experiences at Taft molded my confidence as the young gay man I am today.

HELPING YOUTH FIND A "QUEER VOICE"

As Victor's words illustrate, silence is a reality for LGBTQ youth in schools all over the country. Even in schools with gay-straight alliances, large populations of "out" students, and schoolwide events such as the National Day of Silence to call attention to the need for LGBTQ individuals' voices to be heard, many students do not feel safe or comfortable voicing the LGBTQ aspects of their identities. In previous research I have conducted with LGBTQ adolescents, I have found that the silencing of LGBTQ youth in schools takes many forms: not feeling free to raise their hand in class, not having the opportunity to discuss or study LGBTQ issues, being held to different standards of self-expression than "straight" students (everything from clothing to holding hands with a same-sex boyfriend or girlfriend). In my 2013 book *In a Queer Voice*, I examine both this silencing and the ways educators help LGBTQ students build resistance to it. In so doing, these educators help young people develop what I refer to as a "queer voice." Making deliberate use of the word *queer*, I define a young person's queer voice as one that defiantly challenges traditional notions about gender and sexuality. Youth with a strong queer voice speak their hearts and minds, and they assert their right to live as LGBTQ individuals with authenticity, dignity, and pride.[13]

The educators profiled in this chapter all represent different strategies for helping LGBTQ youth find their unique voices. In the book discussion group at Osceola High School, students are able to read and discuss literature that mirrors aspects of their identities often silenced in the school curriculum. The power of literature to open up previously silenced queer voices is evident in Joan F. Kaywell's edited book, *Dear Author: Letters of Hope*. Kaywell shares letters written to young adult authors by teenage readers who found aspects of their lives—many of which they felt they couldn't talk about with anyone—mirrored in literature. In a letter to Nancy Garden, author of the young adult novel *Annie on My Mind*, which centers on a teenage girl's strong attraction to another girl, a fifteen-year-old reader wrote: "Before reading *Annie on My Mind*, I have never felt like a book spoke to 'me' before. It was an unbelievable relief, and it convinced me that I wasn't destined to live a life of solitude and isolation. It is that feeling, that I can someday fall in love—that I will someday be happy—that made this book great for me. Someday, I can truly believe and it is okay to believe, there will be an Annie in my life. It gives me hope."[14]

Ken Jackson's group counseling sessions at Decatur High School represent another way school-based adults can help LGBTQ youth break their silence and find a queer voice. As discussed at other points in this book, gay-straight alliances can be life-saving oases and serve as sites for leadership development, education, open discussion, and sometimes "coming out." By definition, however, they are not "LGBTQ-only" spaces. Even in GSAs, coming out as lesbian, gay, bisexual, transgender, or queer can feel risky for some students, and they may also need another kind of support group in which the fact that they are LGBTQ is assumed. The opportunity to, as one of the students profiled in *In a Queer Voice* puts it, "just talk" can help give LGBTQ youth an outlet to express any stresses or anxieties associated with homophobia or transphobia in a positive and supportive setting—an alternative to some of the self-destructive coping mechanisms, such as substance abuse and other self-harming behaviors, to which this population is especially vulnerable.[15]

Counseling groups for LGBTQ youth can take many forms, from relatively unstructured places where students can "just talk" to more structured, curriculum-based groups founded in research on strength building and the development of coping strategies. Catherine Griffith, an assistant professor in the counselor education program at the University of Massachusetts–Amherst, has developed an evidence-based group counseling curriculum for use with LGBTQ youth. In a randomized, controlled pilot study in which thirty-four youth participated in the group counseling sessions for eight weeks, Griffith found significant reductions in suicidal thoughts and behaviors and improved coping skills among the group participants, and comparisons to a control group point to the program itself as a significant contributing factor. Although she is still evaluating various aspects of the program, Griffith says that, based on participant evaluations, exercises in "positive reframing," in which young people learn to develop new perspectives on life challenges, show particular promise. On a more basic level, Griffith also found in her postgroup evaluations that simply hearing the perspectives of other LGBTQ youth was an important benefit for participants: "Just having the feelings they're going through be normalized, knowing that there are other people going through some of the things they're going through, was one of the most therapeutic parts of the experience."[16]

Just as knowing other LGBTQ youth who share similar experiences can have therapeutic benefits, knowing LGBTQ adults can help students develop a positive image of what psychologists Hazel Markus and Paula Nurius have called "possible selves."[17] As an out gay man, Jackson seems able to draw on his affinity with students' experiences in a way that brings their voices out in the counseling group. Developing a relationship with an LGBTQ adult at school who can serve as a mentor and role model has been shown to help build the resilience of LGBTQ youth.[18]

Marginalization of LGBTQ youth of color, however, can be an especially problematic issue even in schools with LGBTQ-supportive staff and programming such as gay-straight alliances. As researcher Maria

Gonzalez noted in her interview study with school counselors in the South, issues associated with race and religion can intersect in the lives of LGBTQ youth in ways that are important for school counselors to understand:

> Four of the ten [interview] participants who served as GSA co-sponsors explicitly noted that very few or no students of color were involved in the club and those who did attend meetings seldom actively contributed . . . Additionally, only one participant recalled specific conversations related to black students' negotiations of their racial and sexual identities . . . Perhaps most notably, participants expressed that the intersection of sexual orientation with religion and cultural beliefs was a more frequently discussed topic among LGBT students of color than race, both in GSA meetings and during individual counseling sessions.[19]

Yet, as the work of "openly straight" longtime GSA advisor and mentor Bridget Brownell illustrates, teachers do not have to be working in a counseling setting—nor do they need to be LGBTQ themselves or from the same racial or ethnic background as their students—to make a powerful connection. As I discovered in the *In a Queer Voice* research, which followed some participants longitudinally through follow-up interviews conducted as many as ten years after high school, the work of caring educators can affect the lives of LGBTQ individuals well into adulthood. A connection a young person makes through a piece of literature, a conversation with a counselor who points them toward an LGBTQ-supportive college, or the advice of a caring teacher can have lasting impact.

CHAPTER 7

Making It Elementary

I F TOPICS RELATED TO SEXUAL ORIENTATION and gender nonconformity are controversial in some districts, that controversy is even greater when the students involved are in elementary school. New York City education officials learned this in the 1990s, when the city's board of education published the guide *Children of the Rainbow*, which encouraged teaching about diverse family structures, including those headed by gay and lesbian parents.[1] One program designed for elementary schools that has come under fire from conservative groups and community members more recently is Welcoming Schools, a program of the Human Rights Campaign Foundation. This chapter profiles the Welcoming Schools approach and the work of a third-grade teacher in Washington State who both uses it in her classroom and has begun training other teachers in her building in its implementation. It also highlights two additional approaches created by individual educators, one an arts-based curriculum in Washington State and the other a literature-based course that grew out of a Chicago teacher's observations of her students' own biases about gender and sexual orientation.

THE WELCOMING SCHOOLS APPROACH

Welcoming Schools is a resource guide that includes lesson plans, professional development materials, family education and community-building activities, and other materials designed to help teachers create lessons in three broad areas: family diversity, gender stereotypes, and the harmful effects of bullying. Despite the fact that Welcoming Schools is limited to these three foci, conservative parents, community members, and groups have charged that the program engages students in discussions about sexuality long before they are ready and, in so doing, circumvents the rights of parents to talk to their children about these issues how and when they choose. In 2008, when Minneapolis was one of a handful of cities in which the Welcoming Schools program was being piloted, a group called the Minnesota Family Council posted a statement on its website that had originally been read by a Minneapolis parent to the city's school board. Excerpts from the statement included the following: "[W]e stand with the District and our school in wanting to address the bullying and name calling issues, including the bullying and name calling of GLBT children and their families. However, in doing so we retain the rights as parents to expect our schools not to interfere with our freedom to teach our children our individual beliefs and values, whatever they may be . . ."[2]

Tarah Fleming, education director for Our Family Coalition and expert trainer for the California region of Welcoming Schools, refutes the claim that the program oversteps the line between schooling and parenting. She says that its three strands—family diversity, gender stereotypes, and bullying prevention—have been chosen deliberately to reflect the diverse reality of elementary students' families and to address the problem of gender-biased bullying that often begins in the early elementary grades. Addressing these issues head-on—teaching students at age-appropriate points in their development about the specific kinds of language and behaviors that are hurtful—is required not only to make schools welcoming for elementary school students but also to circumvent the escalation of bias and sexuality-based harassment that continues into middle and high school: "Telling kids to be nice to each other isn't enough. You have to be specific," Fleming says. "So much of the lack of safety in schools is based on gender-biased bullying. This is true for all levels of schooling and goes up into high school with things like sexual harassment and date rape. We have an obligation to do this work in an early, proactive way, in preK–5."

Moreover, the diversity of families from which US students come has many dimensions beyond parents' gender and sexual orientation. According to data cited by Welcoming Schools:

- Almost 2.5 million fathers in the United States are the primary caregivers of their children.
- More than 1.8 million US children are adopted, and almost 40 percent of those children are of a different race, culture, or ethnicity from their parents.
- 16 percent of children live in blended families including stepparents and step- or half-siblings.
- Over 4 million children identify as being of more than one race.
- Almost one-quarter of children have at least one parent who was born in a country other than the United States.
- In every US county, there are gay- and lesbian-headed households.
- In rural states, such as Wyoming and Alaska, and in southern states, households headed by same-sex couples are more likely to have children than same-sex households in other states.[3]

The Welcoming Schools guide includes lesson plans that address these topics through a variety of pedagogical approaches and at various grade levels. For example, lessons on family diversity focus on the fact that families are not always headed by one mother and one father but can also include those headed by same-sex couples as well as foster, one-parent, grandparent-headed, blended, adoptive, and other kinds of families. Lesson plans for this strand include the interdisciplinary "What Is a Family?" and an art project called "Family Quilt." The lessons on gender address issues such as gender stereotyping in children's books and, for older children, in television and other media. The lessons related to name calling address not only slurs related to gender and sexuality but also those associated with race, religion, and other aspects of identity. These lessons have names such as "Words That Hurt and Words That Heal" and "Making Decisions: Ally or Bystander," and teachers are supported in having these conversations with students through glossaries that define words related to LGBTQ identities and family diversity at several levels. (There is a glossary for students in grades K–3, another for students in grades 4–5, and a third for having discussions with parents and community members. In addition to words such as *gay* and *transgender*, students are introduced to terms such as *interfaith family*, *birth mother*, and *foster parent*.)

Fleming works to educate a variety of constituencies who want to make elementary schools more inclusive through the Welcoming Schools approach: parents who want to advocate for more inclusive programming in their children's schools, teachers who need lesson ideas and technical assistance with implementation, and principals who want to lead more inclusive schools but need help managing potential opposition. One of the arguments Fleming drives home to the people with whom she consults is that inclusive programming like Welcoming Schools complements—rather than diverts attention away from—a focus on academic achievement. "What [Welcoming Schools teachers] are doing is legal, developmentally appropriate, and absolutely tied to the skills children need in the twenty-first century," she says. "When children feel safe in school and they feel appreciated, they do better."

To demonstrate the complementarity of inclusive schooling with government-mandated requirements, Welcoming Schools has explicitly aligned many of its lesson plans with Common Core State Standards for English language arts and the National Council for Social Studies curriculum standards.

Evaluation of the Welcoming Schools program is in its early stages, but preliminary data from the first year of the three-year pilot program, which was implemented in twelve schools in California, Massachusetts, and Minnesota, showed some encouraging results:

- Whereas 52 percent of teachers in the pilot schools said fear of parental dissatisfaction was a primary obstacle to their addressing topics related to sexual orientation and family diversity in the classroom prior to implementation, only 28 percent had this concern afterward.

- 60 percent of educators in the pilot schools said they observed an improvement in the schools' overall "climate around diversity" from the beginning to the end of the pilot year.
- Whereas more than half of teachers in September of the pilot year said they felt a "personal lack of training and resources" around addressing LGBTQ issues, that number was down to 30 percent by May.[4]

ONE TEACHER'S EXPERIENCE WITH WELCOMING SCHOOLS

Kimmie Fink, a third-grade teacher at Polk Elementary School in Puyallup, Washington, has used Welcoming Schools resources in her classroom for two years and was recently trained by the organization as a facilitator for her school building so that she could share the resources and approaches with her colleagues. One of the resources she uses in her coaching sessions is a tip sheet for teachers called "What Do You Say to 'That's So Gay'?" Countering the perception that anti-LGBTQ language is an issue only in middle and high school, Fink says the putdown "that's so gay" (which children and teenagers often use to indicate they believe something is "stupid" or otherwise negative) is ubiquitous in elementary schools. "I have third graders who say that like it's nothing," she notes. "The worst thing a teacher can do is ignore it, because they [students] really don't know what they're saying. They don't intend to be malicious."

Recommendations on the tip sheet for educating about, rather than ignoring, this kind of language include:

- If you have been hearing the phrase "that's gay" used to mean that something is bad or stupid, take the time during a class meeting to make sure that your students know what *gay* means and know why it is hurtful to use it as an insult.
- Be clear with students that when they use the word *gay* in a negative way they are being disrespectful. Be clear that using the phrase

"that's so gay" is hurtful to other students who may have family members and friends who are gay.

- Provide accurate information. For the youngest students, keep it simple. For example, "the word *gay* describes a man and a man who love each other, or a woman and a woman who love each other."[5]

Fink, who has taught for thirteen years, says she always wanted to address anti-LGBTQ language with her elementary students, but without the tools or language she is now learning through the program, all she used to feel when students said homophobic or sexist things to one another was anger: "Before Welcoming Schools, whenever a third grader said something like that, I just got mad. I didn't know what else to do." Having the Welcoming Schools materials as a resource, Fink says, has helped her move from a place of frustration and perceived helplessness to one in which she is now able to use such incidents as teachable moments.

To introduce the concept of being an "upstander"—someone who stands up to bullies and speaks out for the rights of others—Fink uses the Welcoming Schools materials around the children's book *One* by Kathryn Otoshi, in which the quiet color blue is picked on by the "hothead" color red until the other colors learn to speak up.[6] Another exercise from the Welcoming Schools guide that Fink uses in her classroom involves taking a construction paper heart and crumpling it, then opening it up again. Fink then asks her students, "Is it the same as it was before, or is it different?" Students are able to recognize that, even though the heart is still in one piece, it doesn't look the way it did before—a metaphor for the way that bullying and insulting language can have lasting effects even if the people targeted by them appear to be okay afterward. "After an exercise like that, kids will share things that have happened to them that have been hurtful," says Fink. "It really opens up conversations."

A PARENT CREATES A "WELCOMING SCHOOL" FOR HER CHILD

As valuable as the classroom conversations that emerge from Welcoming Schools work might be, people who advocate for this kind of inclusion in elementary classrooms quickly learn that not all school administrators feel ready to take on the potential opposition that might emerge from the program's frank discussion of anti-LGBTQ language and other issues. Parent Lisa J. Keating was turned down when she requested that her child's school implement Welcoming Schools several years ago: "Welcoming Schools takes a bold approach to language. It scares some administrators," she observes. Yet rather than simply take no for an answer, Keating created her own curriculum, which she now teaches at Geiger Montessori school, a public elementary school in Tacoma, Washington.

An arts-based curriculum designed for three multigrade groupings (prekindergarten to kindergarten, grades 1–3, and grades 4–5), "Allies in Action" doesn't explicitly address the issues of LGBTQ students or anti-LGBTQ language, but it opens discussions among elementary school students through art-based projects around seven core themes:

- Respect
- Courage
- Trust
- Honesty
- Compassion
- Bravery
- Love

The idea, Keating says, is for children to explore each of these abstract concepts through tangible art projects and to reflect on how they connect to one another. (How is trust related to honesty? How can you have respect without compassion?) She then engages students in discussions about how all these qualities together point toward a key theme of the program: what it takes to be an *ally* to their peers, especially those who might be subject to bullying. Keating describes one art activity, the "ally chain," as having prompted discussion about multiple levels of diversity among students:

Each classroom participates in a group discussion on the character qualities and empathy in relation to being an ally. During this lesson, the students are given colored strips of card stock and markers. Each strip represents a link. I explain that every student is a member of Geiger's [elementary school] community. They are instructed to draw pictures or words that show what it means to be an ally. Students often write phrases, [or] draw scenes where someone was an ally to them or they were an ally to someone else.

One of the most memorable experiences was with a Muslim girl in third grade. She looked very uncomfortable and wasn't writing or drawing anything for ten minutes. After checking in with her a couple times and not getting anywhere, I privately asked the teacher if she was able to write in English. She had really struggled with English, especially in writing. A light bulb went off and I asked this student if she could write one of the links in Arabic. Completely surprised she replied, "I can *do* that?" The rest of the class was very excited and fascinated to learn about Arabic. This organically created an opportunity for this girl to teach her peers about her culture.

Now that Keating has taught the curriculum for two years, the ally theme has caught on with her older students so strongly that they requested permission to start an afterschool Allies in Action club. In some respects like an elementary-level version of a GSA, the group, which now has about fifteen members ages ten to twelve, has engaged in school climate improvement projects such as creating posters with messages about being an ally and performing skits for a school assembly that show the effects of hurtful words on students who are bullied.

The inspiration for all this work, Keating says, is her own "gender-fluid" child, who transitioned to the use of a girl's name at age ten. Although Keating feels fortunate that her child has always had affirming teachers and that her school administration supports the arts curriculum and other measures that challenge gender stereotypes at school, she notes that most elementary teachers and administrators deal with issues such as name calling and bullying only when problems arise. This "crisis management" approach, she says, places gender-nonconforming students at risk: "It's all crisis management, and there's very little proactive work in elementary schools, which is where the social hierarchy [among students] starts. If we don't do things in elementary school, it's going to continue to be crisis management."

The biggest crisis, warns Keating, is the dramatic rate of suicidal behavior among transgender and gender-nonconforming youth, even as young as elementary school. Suicide is the third leading cause of death among early adolescents (children ages ten to fourteen) according to the Centers for Disease Control and Prevention.[7] And, given the fact that transgender and gender-nonconforming youth are often among the most frequently isolated, marginalized, and bullied at school, these are statistics of which Keating and other parents of gender-nonconforming children are well aware: "For those of us parenting gender-diverse youth, that's a reality. It's not a matter of if we're going to have an elementary school kid attempt suicide, it's when."

EXTRACTING LESSONS FROM LIFE IN THE CLASSROOM

Connecting with an organization like Welcoming Schools or working with a teacher such as Keating through an established curriculum is one way to address issues related to bullying, family diversity, and gender stereotypes with elementary students. But educators without budgets for outside consultants, or who face opposition to such programs from school leaders, can take more home-grown, investigative approaches to debunking gender stereotypes and combating sexist, homophobic, and transphobic language and bullying among their students.[8]

Second-grade bilingual teacher Alexandria Hollett began what became a two-year pair of action research projects at Chicago's Shields Elementary School, a preK–8 school located in the city's Brighton Park neighborhood, in the 2011–2012 school year. A large percentage of Hollett's second-graders (97 percent) were Latino, and more than 99 percent came from low-income families. At the time Hollett conducted her research, Shields was one of the city's largest elementary schools, with an average of eight teachers per grade level.

As described by Richard Sagor in the book *Guiding School Improvement with Action Research*, the practice of action research involves a cyclical process whereby a single teacher or group of teachers identifies an issue in their classroom(s) they'd like to know more about, collects and analyzes data, then takes "informed action" to address the issue as suggested by the research results.[9] (The informed action then leads to further data collection, analysis, and implementation.) Hollett received funding from the nonprofit Chicago Foundation for Education, which provides grants to Chicago teachers to conduct action research in their classrooms over the course of one academic year. Originally, Hollett did not set out to conduct a research project related to homophobia or perceptions related to issues of gender nonconformity; her original interest was to examine whether and how students used conflict resolution strategies to solve interpersonal struggles. Hollett began using various research protocols—such as focused observations, analysis of student conversations, and formal and informal interviews—to understand how her students were resolving the conflicts that arose among them. During her pursuit of this broader research question, however, issues related to students' statements and perceptions about sexual orientation and gender became so prominent that she felt compelled to refine her focus:

> I became very interested in a few dominant trends present in the classroom in regard to what types of conflict were occurring, and I noticed that the majority of issues involved disagreement over appropriate gender roles and/or sexual orientation. The reigning classroom insult was to call students gay, and most confrontations or tensions had to do with students not wanting to work with peers of differing genders and/or making fun of nonconforming students. After Christmas break, my research focus shifted to explicitly exploring these two aspects of identity.[10]

In response to what she was observing, Hollett created a gender roles unit whereby she and her students analyzed texts and media representations of celebrities and other individuals and discussed both the explicit and implicit messages about gender that were embedded in these representations. From listening to student conversations, both formally and informally, she noticed that even her second graders viewed what they saw in the media through homophobic and sexist lenses:

> My students were obsessed with celebrities, particularly Justin Bieber. There was one day where some of my students (girls) were talking about him and a group of boys started making fun of him, explicitly calling him gay. I asked the group of students if they knew what the word *gay* meant and one responded, "It's when boys want to kiss other boys" and the rest of the group broke into grossed-out laughter. At other moments, they accused each other of being gay when they were upset. Most frequently, however, jokes were made about girls not being able to do certain things or students being unwilling to work together as a result of gender differences.

In consultation with another second-grade teacher at her school who was well versed in children's literature, Hollett selected books, mostly picture books, that addressed issues related to gender, stereotypes, and bullying to read and discuss with students. Through this unit, she addressed both students' literacy needs as well as the books' thematic focus on perceptions associated with gender and/or sexual orientation. In this way, Hollett says she was able to attend simultaneously to students' literacy development, social and emotional growth, and state and city curriculum requirements:

> I used children's books with my second graders for literacy purposes as well as content. For example, when reading a particular text we would not only discuss the messages, themes, or author's intent but also the structure of writing, figurative language, phonetics, whatever was relevant for the fluency and literacy component of the week or month. We held literature circles during which we got more into the meat, so to speak, of the text. During these times we would discuss our reactions as readers, complicate or extend our thinking, challenge what the author seemed to be proposing, or discuss new ideas.

Through the literature, we interrogated stereotypes about gender and sexuality. We looked at the ways in which books and movies portray the options available to members of different groups, and through a few key anchor texts, such as *10,000 Dresses, And Tango Makes Three, King and King, Christian the Hugging Lion, The Sissy Duckling,* and *Olivia,* we explored family structures, what it means to have a meaningful relationship, what it means to be free to be yourself, and how society tries to teach us to judge people or put people (and ourselves) into constricting boxes.[11] All of our activities were aligned to the Common Core State Standards, so I was satisfying academic requirements as well as engaging in social/emotional/justice learning.

To explore these texts and topics, Hollett had "a lot of Socratic seminar–type discussions" with her second graders. Over time, she noted that these discussions were associated with greater awareness and more self-monitoring among students with regard to negative language and stereotypes about gender or sexual orientation. Another outcome was that her students decided to challenge the usual practice of lining up in boy/girl rows to walk through the building. Instead, they chose to line up according to things that they liked such as colors, superheroes (for example, Superman versus Batman), sports and games, and other preferences. As a conversation with one of her students illustrates, many were beginning to see the differences among them in ways that went beyond gender:

> *Hollett:* Am I remembering correctly that you prefer to line up by choices instead of boys and girls?
> *Student:* Yes.
> *Hollett:* Why do you like to do that?
> *Student:* Because I can see that many people like different stuff and because it's fun.[12]

Hollett says her students also voted to "outlaw" use of the word *gay* as a put-down in the classroom and, when she asked students at the end of the year to rate their favorite of the books they had read throughout the class, eight of the top ten choices came from their unit on gender.

Although the action research project Hollett conducted at Shields took place only in one classroom over one year—she changed schools and grade levels within the Chicago system the following year—it illustrates how engaging students in critical discussions about gender, homophobia, and related issues can have a stronger impact than a teacher-imposed "zero tolerance" policy against bullying. In addition, her work challenges the perception that second graders are too young to discuss issues related to gender and homophobia, because they were already doing so without the benefit of adult guidance:

> By second grade, my students were already completely indoctrinated into prescribed notions of normativity and were incredibly cognizant of difference or nonconformance. We had to actively engage in work that sought to break apart those ideas, to discern why we felt or thought certain things, and to think critically about the legitimacy of those thoughts/feelings. If I had just said, "OK, here's the rule— no hate language, everyone plays together regardless of gender" that would have been a start. But I doubt very much that it would have been super-impactful on their development as empathic and civically minded humans.

Continuing the Project with Sixth Graders

The next school year, Hollett taught sixth-grade reading and writing at Patrick Henry Elementary School, in Chicago's Albany Park neighborhood. Although a much smaller school than Shields, with about 660 students, Patrick Henry also served a predominantly Latino population (about 78 percent), and 96 percent of the students came from families classified as low-income.

Having conducted the action research project at Shields the previous year, Hollett says she wanted to see if issues related to gender and homophobia played as large a role in student interactions as they did for the second graders at Shields. She conducted a student survey as well as formal and informal observations and interviews and learned "very quickly" that these issues were even more salient for the sixth graders than for the younger students. The sixth graders reported that homophobic language and bullying were common in school, and it was clear from their comments that, as emerging adolescents, they were preoccupied with gender roles and stereotypes. At the sixth-grade level, some students also openly shared that they knew LGBTQ people. In response to her findings, and as she had done with her second-grade class, Hollett approached most of her exploration of gender- and sexuality-related topics with her sixth graders through literature:

> We read a lot of literature by "alternative" voices and got pretty deep into discussing real-life scenarios of knowing people who were queer as well as talking about the fact that schools are not often safe spaces for kids who are gender nonconforming or identify as gay or lesbian. Apart from doing much of the same things as the second graders (just at a more sophisticated level), my students also conducted in-school research to see whether stereotypes about gender and sexuality were present in more than just our classroom. Groups of students went into my colleagues' rooms and asked the younger students in the school to give them ideas for what they perceived to be appropriate gender roles. After they collected the data we looked at similarities and differences, cross-referenced the data with other research conducted by organizations like GLSEN, for example, and held literature/research circles to discuss our findings.

Much of the literature Hollett read with her sixth graders was either written by LGBTQ-identified writers or those who challenge gender- and sexuality-based norms and oppression in their work. For example, during a poetry slam unit, students studied the work of spoken word artist and writer Ivan Coyote and poet Andrea Gibson, both of whose work challenges the traditional man/woman gender binary. Since she was able to take the discussion of gender to a more sophisticated level with the sixth graders, Hollett says she discussed the gender spectrum and transgender identity with her students, and one result was their own rethinking of the custom of lining up to walk through the building by gender. To illustrate the idea that "boys and girls" is a binary concept that does not represent the full gender continuum, the students came up with a new policy to walk through the building in three lines instead of the usual two. As is usually the case with action research, Hollett's sixth-grade project resulted both in what she considered successful outcomes and in aspects of the work she would do differently on another round:

> My feelings about the success of my unit at Henry are pretty mixed. On the one hand, I don't feel like it was as successful academically as I wanted it to be; students engaged in critical thinking and analysis, but the unit wasn't as tight or intentional as it had been in my second-grade classroom . . . However, I think of that year very fondly because I saw changes in my students regarding their beliefs about what was "normal" or "cool." We had plenty of conflicts, but they weren't overwhelmingly about gender and sexuality. One of my students came out to me toward the end of the year, and many more were open about being accepting of gender/sexuality variance. When my students were tasked with writing a letter to President Obama to encourage him to pay particular attention to a current issue of their choice, many of them chose to advocate for national recognition of queer relationships. Queer rights, histories, and voices were integrated into all units, but students often had choices about what aspects of justice issues they felt most compelled to explore.

Like the majority of teachers in the schools where Welcoming Schools conducted its pilot study, Hollett says parental objections were a significant concern of hers when she began addressing LGBTQ- and gender-related issues with her elementary school students. Ultimately, however, Hollett says getting past these trepidations was necessary not only to show respect for families and for the work but also to be prepared in the event any objections arose:

Although I was very wary about being completely open regarding the work we were doing in class, I ultimately decided to be as transparent as possible. So before embarking on what could be seen to be controversial subjects of study, I sent home a letter to parents explaining what we were doing and the impetus for doing so. Every parent had my phone number from day one (students, too) and I had an open-door policy. In terms of pushback from parents, I experienced no opposition at all, however.

The most important advice I would give is to be transparent. It's not possible to please everyone at once, but if you're going to tackle difficult topics, it's a sign of respect to do so in the full light of day. This not only speaks to your integrity as an educator, but it also protects you in the event that there would be a real problem that arises.

ARTICULATING THE NEED FOR INCLUSIVE ELEMENTARY SCHOOLS

As demonstrated by the objections Minneapolis educators faced when Welcoming Schools was introduced there, articulating the need for programs like it—and explaining what they do and do not teach students—is critical to their introduction, sustenance, and success. As discussed further in the next chapter, being conversant with a school's or district's mission statement and stated commitments to priorities such as a safe climate, inclusiveness, or universal achievement can help educators make the case that lessons related to gender, family diversity, and LGBTQ-based bullying are consistent with these core values. If the district has already established an overall focus on multiculturalism, this can also serve as a useful foundation for arguments that LGBTQ-inclusive programming fits within that larger framework.[13] Articulating the connection to a school district's broader mission can be especially important for elementary programs, on which educators might be more likely to relent in the face of real or anticipated pressure from administrators, parents, or community members.

As education researcher Elizabeth Meyer explains, much of the objection to LGBTQ-themed topics at the elementary level stems from the misconception that discussing these topics amounts to talking about sex with young children:

> Many parents and professional educators do not immediately see the relevance of issues of gender and sexual diversity in elementary school classrooms. Unfortunately, many of these critics incorrectly believe that talking about diverse sexualities means that there will be explicit conversations about sexual behaviors. In elementary schools, this is generally not age-appropriate, nor is it recommended. Issues of gender and sexuality affect everyone and do not only impact students after they have reached puberty. The two main issues of gender and sexual diversity that are most relevant in the lives of young children are those related to gender role expectations and parenting and family relationships.
>
> Gender roles are taught at school. When children enter pre-school and kindergarten they are learning much about gender codes and what is expected of them if they are a boy or girl. They are often fixated on "what boys do" and "what girls wear" and most try very hard to follow these rules.[14]

To "help students feel valued and included in all of their gender diversity," Meyer recommends practices that touch on themes similar to those that undergird the work highlighted in this chapter:

1. When teaching about careers be sure to have images and role models that show men and women in a variety of career roles.
2. Be sure your class library and play centers include books and toys for all interests that aren't labeled or segregated by gender.
3. Avoid having your students line up by sex: try using other organizing categories such as first name, last name, height, or birth month.

4. When talking about families and home life, be sure to talk about the various roles and responsibilities that parents may have. Avoid talking about what "mommies do" and "daddies do"— especially since many students may have only one parent, or may be living with a grandparent or other caregiver.

5. When choosing stories to read in class make sure you have a wide selection of stories of girls and boys as main characters and that show girls as lead characters and boys as caring and supportive friends.

6. When choosing diverse representations of gender and sexuality in stories and images, pay attention to including people from different racial and ethnic backgrounds.[15]

As Welcoming Schools articulates in a section of its resource guide, "Responding to Some Concerns About Being LGBT Inclusive" (see exhibit 7.1 in appendix A), its lessons related to LGBTQ bullying also touch on topics that are meaningful in *all* elementary students' lives. Children are often subject to a variety of slurs (some of which relate to LGBTQ identities, and some to race, gender, and other factors) even before they understand their meaning:

> Students use the phrase "that's so gay" long before they know what the word "gay" means. Anti-LGBT or gender-related put-downs are among the most commonly heard slurs in school environments. When educators address the use of the word "gay," they are not introducing either the topic or the vocabulary.
>
> When name-calling and put-downs are discussed it is important for educators to explicitly discuss the kinds of words that students are using. Words like gay or queer or sissy are words that hurt their classmates and friends. In these discussions on name-calling it is respect that is being discussed.[16]

In California, Fleming makes sure that the educators with whom she consults understand how inclusive programs like Welcoming Schools help meet state mandates. There, all publicly funded schools must submit *local control and accountability plans* (LCAPs), in which officials describe how they intend to meet annual goals for all students and conduct specific activities related to priorities identified at the state and local levels. Fleming explains that for California, all LCAP formulas must include a school climate component and articulation of how schools will address the needs of three target groups identified as underserved in the state: children in foster care, second-language learners, and low-income children. All of these groups are widely represented among the state's LGBTQ population, she notes: "Queer families tend to be poor, there are a lot of LGBTQ kids in foster care, and there are a lot of immigrant LGBTQ kids. They're inherently in these three groups." While government mandates obviously vary from state to state and community to community, the foundation to articulate a case for LGBTQ-inclusive elementary programming might already exist in these kinds of policy requirements.

Data can be another important source of support for articulating the need for inclusive elementary schools. Both national data and classroom- and school-based data like Hollett's support what many elementary teachers know from experience: students at the elementary level are already steeped in traditional notions about gender and are well aware of language related to race, religion, and LGBTQ identities that can be used to bully other students. Moreover, gender-nonconforming children are among the most frequently bullied by their peers in elementary schools. Yet while most teachers know these things from observation if not from research, the Welcoming Schools data shows that: 1) without training, teachers are reluctant to address these topics with young children; 2) lack of knowledge and access to resources can be a major obstacle to their doing so.[17] As researcher Teresa Bouley has found, although most elementary school teachers are well versed in children's literature, most cannot name a single book that depicts LGBTQ characters.[18]

Hollett's recommendations for transparency may be particularly relevant to work at the elementary level because of the many misconceptions surrounding it. Educators should obviously consider context when making these decisions—it may be easier for a teacher to avoid controversy in Chicago than at a rural elementary school in the Bible Belt—but the focus on core values as articulated previously may be a useful centerpiece for family, school board, or community discussions in any context.

CHAPTER 8

Where Do You Start?

Beginning with Core Values— but Not Ending There

I HAVE WRITTEN THIS BOOK in the belief that there are many teachers, administrators, and staff working in the United States who are ready and eager to make their schools more than "safe" for their LGBTQ students but don't know where to begin. If the schools and educators profiled in chapters 1 through 7 demonstrate two fundamental truths about the path toward making schools more LGBTQ-inclusive, they are as follows:

- Context matters—a lot—but it is not destiny. Educators can effect change in any context as long as they understand the school and community in which they are working and the needs of their own particular students.
- In addition to an awareness of context, being an effective advocate for LGBTQ-inclusive school programming requires persistence, courage, and a good strategy.

This final case study focuses on a school in Indiana where, compared to some of the other schools profiled in this book, educators have been advancing the cause of the LGBTQ inclusion for a relatively short time. Yet the progress they have made in less than five years, in a politically conservative community where many might not have thought such work possible, demonstrates how a strategic focus on fundamental community values and core school district beliefs can minimize early roadblocks and provide a useful foundation from which to build further success.

RAINBOW FLAGS IN A RED-STATE SCHOOL

Indiana is widely regarded in political circles as a highly conservative state, consistently "red" even in elections when most other midwestern states have tended to turn blue. The state is currently one of a handful where a "religious freedom" law, which some say protects business owners and managers who wish to discriminate against LGBTQ people on religious grounds, is in effect. And the Indianapolis suburb of Avon, about fifteen miles from downtown, is in many ways a microcosm of the state in which it is located, reliably conservative both politically and religiously. Results for the last two presidential elections showed that Republican votes in Hendricks County, where Avon is located and which follows typical county patterns, outnumbered Democratic votes by a ratio of 2 to 1, and in some local races, there are no Democratic candidates on the ballot. The area is home to mainline Protestant denominations alongside a significant number of evangelical ministries and growing Catholic, Muslim, and Hindu communities.

Unlike other Indianapolis suburbs that have seen rapidly rising property values, however, housing prices in Avon have stayed relatively affordable, resulting in booming population growth and a high school population that increases by 150 to 200 students every year and now stands at 2,900. Though still more than 70 percent white, the student population has also become increasingly diverse in the last decade with regard to race and ethnicity: about 10 percent African American, 8 percent Latino, and 4 percent Asian American. Moreover, about 4 percent of the district's nine thousand or so students speak English as a second language.

In this context, one might not expect school administrators to count the high school's gay-straight alliance as one of its strongest organizations, much less to announce this proudly and publicly—yet this is precisely what is taking place in this conservative town, county, and state. And, like those of the town in which it is located, the changes at Avon High School have happened quickly and in impressive numbers.

Although gay-straight alliances have been around since the late 1980s and began to proliferate around the country in the 1990s and 2000s, Avon's GSA got a relatively late start. It was founded in 2011, the result of years of student discontent that gradually gave way to activism. "I had had students talking to me for two or three years about how they wish they had one [a GSA]," recalls English teacher Dawn Fable-Lindquist. Fable-Lindquist believes that students chose her as a potential GSA advisor because she didn't shy away from LGBTQ issues in her English classes and "always talked about acceptance of other people" as it related to characters in the literature students read. At first, though, Fable-Lindquist says neither she nor the students at Avon thought a GSA could succeed in their conservative community.

Even if Fable-Lindquist thought she could persuade administrators and the school board that the GSA was a good idea, this route was not an option. Well-known schoolwide rules dictated that students, not faculty, were the only ones who could start a club, so she let the students decide when the time was right. And while this regulation seemed an impediment at first, it ultimately proved to be key to the successful effort to start and maintain a GSA.

Outside Inspiration Meets Internal Policy

At Fable-Lindquist's suggestion, a group of five sophomore students attended a leadership conference run by Indiana Youth Group, a statewide organization in Indianapolis that provides support, safe spaces, and leadership training to LGBTQ youth from around the state. At the conference, the Avon students networked with other youth concerned about LGBTQ issues, learned what was happening in other schools, and were inspired by the message that LGBTQ-positive programming was going on in schools around the country, even in Indiana, and was therefore possible at Avon. They started to envision how their school could become more LGBTQ-friendly, and they went to assistant principal

Kellie Rodkey, who coordinates all student activities for the school, to take the first step and apply to start a gay-straight alliance.

For Rodkey, the answer was clear because of long-established criteria and procedures for initiating afterschool organizations, and she treated the request like she would any other inquiry by students who wanted to initiate a club, and as she had done many times before: "I didn't blink an eye; it fit all the criteria. It fulfilled a need, it fell under the school's mission statement, it had a community service component . . ."

The school mission statement reads as follows:

The mission of Avon High School is instruction and learning for all students. It is our responsibility to help students reach their full potential and master challenging curricula. Students will be taught the importance of academic excellence, critical thinking, and communication skills required for the 21st century. In addition, our staff will foster an environment of personal integrity, responsibility, empathy for others, and respect for cultural diversity. In a collaborative effort with colleagues, students, parents, and the community, the Avon High School staff will monitor student achievement through state and local assessments and respond with a systemic plan of intervention to meet the needs of students who are failing to meet rigorous standards.

This is followed on the school website immediately by a diversity statement, which reads as follows:

Diversity is strength, and multicultural experiences are vital components of the educational process. It is the policy of Avon High School to recognize the uniqueness of each individual. Statements or behavior which insult, degrade, or stereotype any other person on the basis of race, gender, handicap, intellectual ability, physical condition, sexual orientation, socio-economic background, ethnic or national origin, or religion are unacceptable. The school community will show consideration for the rights, opinions, and values of all individuals at Avon High School.

Knowing she had the weight of these school mission and diversity statements behind her, Rodkey then instructed the GSA organizers to complete the following standard steps for the student-led initiation of a club:

1. Collect twenty-five student signatures to show sufficient interest.
2. Draft a constitution in keeping with the school's required parameters.
3. Find one or more faculty sponsors.
4. Seek approval by the student government.

The first two requirements had been met (more than one hundred students signed the petition for the club, far more than the required twenty-five), and Fable-Lindquist was already on board, so the student government voted. Its members unanimously approved the GSA.

Although Rodkey had full authority to work with students on starting any afterschool organization, it was important to let the principal and superintendent know that a GSA was coming to Avon High. The administration knew there would be some community opposition (although they overestimated how much), but they also knew they had school, district, and state policy behind them. As Rodkey explains, "I did know it would stir some feelings in the community. We got two parent phone calls, enraged about how we could support this, and the principal simply said we were abiding by school policy and by state law."

Although some school administrators feel a need to meet with community stakeholders before a GSA forms, Rodkey believed such a meeting would have sent the wrong message from the start and might have communicated that this was somehow a "different kind of club." And she saw no reason for it given the established school mission statement and policy: "We've never had a meeting to talk about the gamers' club, the science club, or any other club. Why would we have a meeting to talk about the GSA?" She was backed up in this approach by superintendent Maggie Hoernemann. "We didn't make a big deal out of it—it was business as usual," recalls Hoernemann. "As a result, I think it was, frankly, a nonevent."

Starting and Maintaining the GSA

Using established policies, procedures, and mission statements certainly helped a GSA get approved quickly in this conservative community, but the organizers knew these things couldn't get students to join. The date for the first meeting was set and, even with the large number of signatures the group had collected, Fable-Lindquist and the student organizers were unsure if anyone would actually show up: "We weren't sure if students would feel comfortable coming to meetings, even though we had the signatures. It was one thing to sign the petition, but we thought a lot of students might be afraid to come, because then people might label them as gay, whether they actually were or not." In addition, there were rumblings in the school that some students who were opposed to the club planned to disrupt the first meeting or, at the very least, peek through the door to see who was in the room.

But the students at Avon did more than sign up; they showed up. Along with Fable-Lindquist and coadvisor Jamie Gleissner, more than fifty students and four administrators came to the first meeting. (The administrators were there to show their support but also in case the rumors about disruption, which never materialized, were true.) After this first meeting, the overwhelming response to the GSA forced the group to move to a larger room, and Fable-Lindquist says official GSA membership has held steady at more than sixty every year since its inception, with biweekly attendance fluctuating between thirty-five and fifty students.

One of the keys to the continued success and popularity of the Avon GSA has been, as Fable-Lindquist explains, "varying the meetings and activities so that kids don't get bored." The GSA has marched in the Indianapolis LGBT pride parade (she believes it was the largest high school group in attendance last year), has participated every year since 2012 in the National Day of Silence (whereby students remain silent for the day and communicate nonverbally in their classes to symbolize the silencing of LGBTQ identities in American society), has hosted a costume party with students from neighboring GSAs, and has partnered with other Avon school clubs on various projects. In one such collaboration, the GSA had joint meetings with the creative writing club for a project in which students wrote "coming out" stories, not necessarily about being gay, lesbian, bisexual, transgender, or queer, but about any aspect of their identities they believed they kept "in the closet" from their peers or families.

The GSA has also had guest speakers visit the school to discuss themes important to students in the community. Religious leaders have addressed the GSA to talk about how to integrate spirituality with LGBTQ identity or support as an ally. "There are kids who do want to have a real spiritual life, but they're not sure if that's possible if they are LGBT or even are straight allies," Fable-Lindquist says.

Starting—but Not Ending—with Safety

One of the ways the Avon teachers and administrators believe they have avoided controversy is by framing the GSA and its activities accurately and unapologetically, but also strategically, in the early days of the group. The first year the GSA sponsored a Day of Silence, for example, they framed the purpose largely in terms of school safety and discussed the silencing of LGBTQ individuals in the context of violence and discrimination perpetrated against many marginalized groups. They also focused on an antibullying message, which was consistent with conversations that were already going on at school. At this first Day of Silence, in which more than two hundred students participated, the GSA invited members of the school community to sign an antibullying poster, and people from all over the building—students, teachers, counselors, custodians—were all represented. Now that students and staff understand what the GSA is about and it has been integrated so fully into the school community, Fable-Lindquist says such "strategic marketing" is no longer necessary: "Whereas in our first year we discussed the GSA at freshman orientation in terms of safety and diversity, now our presentation is much more a reflection of what the club is like."

A central theme of the Avon GSA that reinforces the group's deep integration into the school community is the notion of "home." On its web page, called "GSA Home Sweet Home" (which, unlike many GSA websites, is easily accessible via the school's main web page), the proud message, which focuses more on fun and fellowship than safety, reads: "Avon High School's gay-straight alliance is one of the school's largest clubs, with more than 60 members and three faculty advisors! We are a group that welcomes everyone who supports the rights of our LGBTQ students. We focus on support, tolerance and fellowship, together with healthy doses of education and activism!"[1]

Addressing the Needs of Transgender Students

Avon's teachers and administrators have also cited districtwide priorities and goals to advocate for the needs of students who have come out as transgender. A recent school climate audit conducted by the high school administration found that students who identify as transgender were the subgroup who felt the least safe and most marginalized in the school community, and the district has taken several steps to address these issues in response both to the findings of the audit and to the needs and requests of several students and their families.

Working with a transgender student and their family, the district has convened teams every year to ease that student's passage through the system. In the past few years, the high school has converted several faculty restrooms to unisex bathrooms that any student can use without seeking special permission. Students in the high school's broadcasting classes work on public service announcements to help their peers understand transgender issues better. And, in another subtle but meaningful change to long-standing tradition, rather than simply assigning students graduation gowns based on their gender as designated in school records, the high school now allows students to choose their own color garb for the ceremony.

A CULTURE OF CHANGE

One of the factors that seems to have contributed to the recent changes at Avon High School is change itself. With the high school alone gaining 150–200 students per year and becoming more racially, religiously, linguistically, and ethnically diverse all the time, preparing faculty, staff, students, and families for change and diversity had to be central to the school's and the district's plans going forward if it were to continue to succeed, according to Superintendent Hoernemann. She believes the whole district's changing demographics provided fertile soil for change on many fronts: "Our growth was a benefit [to the work on LGBTQ issues], because when there are so many changes to demographics, you almost *have* to embrace change. I've worked in other communities in Indiana where it became very easy to be insular. Here, we are always continuing to learn how to serve our students and families."

The district's major push to embrace the changing dynamics of its community started around 2008, when administrators and the school board met to discuss what they observed as widening cultural gaps between students and parents of color in the community on the one hand and a predominantly white faculty and administration on the other. From the 1998–1999 school year to 2008–2009, total enrollment in the district nearly doubled from around 4,300 to more than 8,300; the percentage of students receiving free or reduced-price lunch also doubled from 9 percent to 18 percent; the percentage of black students went from below 0.5 percent to 8.5 percent; the percentage of Hispanic students went from 1 percent to 5 percent; and the percentage of Asian American students went from 0.7 percent to 3 percent.

In response to these major demographic shifts, the Avon school board and administration took two overarching, macro-level steps that paved the way for more changes in specific areas, including LGBTQ issues. First, they revised the school system's strategic plan to include the following statement among its five tenets: "Establish a climate and culture that embraces all children, families, employees and citizens of the Avon community." (See exhibit 8.1, the latest version of the district's strategic plan, in appendix A.) While such a change may seem purely semantic on one level, the strategic plan drives all major district-level funding and policy decisions. It served as a rationale for Rodkey's instant initial approval of the students' GSA application and serves as a reminder of the district's priorities when potentially controversial decisions like those involving the accommodations for transgender students need to be made. The revisions to the strategic plan also facilitated the second major change, a large-scale professional development effort to provide all faculty, administration, and staff with cultural competence training.

The district hired Gary Howard, author of the book *We Can't Teach What We Don't Know* and one of the country's best-known consultants providing professional development in the area of cultural competence, to conduct a series of four sessions with administrators. The implementation of cultural competence training varies from one school district to another, but the basic principles involve an examination of one's cultural identity and biases across different types of cultural difference. After the initial four sessions with Howard, administrators helped train building-level coordinators. Several of the seven basic components of cultural competence, though they obviously relate to many kinds of cultural difference, have clear relevance to work with LGBTQ youth and issues:

1. Students are affirmed in their cultural connections.
2. Teachers are personally inviting.
3. Learning environments are physically and culturally inviting.
4. Students are reinforced for academic development.
5. Instructional changes are made to accommodate differences in learners.
6. Classroom is managed with firm, consistent, loving control.
7. Interactions stress collectivity as well as individuality.[2]

After what Hoernemann calls "a profound and significant commitment of time and money" to cultural competence training the first few years, a failed referendum in 2011 forced the district to redirect its cultural competence initiative toward more home-grown approaches, relying more on the human resources department to train new hires and on building-level coordinators to carry on the work in their respective schools. But the priorities, as articulated in the strategic plan, had already been set. Hoernemann says the district remains committed to ensuring that all staff—not just teachers and administrators, but all adults who work with students (e.g., secretaries, food service workers, custodians, nurses, counselors, aides, and bus drivers)—learn how to work effectively across difference. A number of building-level initiatives, including the high school climate audit that found transgender students to be particularly ill-served at the school, have emerged out of the building-level cultural competence work happening in the district's schools.

Even given all the progress of the last few years, however, there is plenty of room for additional growth. Fable-Lindquist believes the district needs to move beyond its broad-based approaches to cultural competence and provide targeted professional development about LGBTQ issues, perhaps drawing on Indiana Youth Group as a resource. The district also lacks a coordinated program for the inclusion of LGBTQ issues in curriculum, an issue that Hoernemann says she'd like to look at next. But Avon's firm foundation in core values and principles has helped lay valuable groundwork for future progress.

FOCUSING ON THE CORE

Although Avon is still clearly at the beginning of its journey toward being a school system that affirms LGBTQ students across many aspects of school life, it serves as an example of the kind of rapid change that is possible when schools draw strategically on structures, policies, and community factors that already exist to address broader priorities. The school's clear-cut, unambiguous policy on the process for initiating student clubs—as well as a mission statement that prioritized respect for diversity—made the introduction of the GSA a "nonevent," in the words of Superintendent Hoernemann. Moreover, the community's rapidly changing demographics created an opportunity whereby educators and the community were able to see LGBTQ-positive programming within the context of a focus on multiculturalism, as these broader changes required.

Teachers, administrators, and staff usually work under a set of essential beliefs that drive their schools, at least in theory, even while these might be subject to many compromises necessitated by the day-to-day realities of their work. Often, core values have been articulated for an entire school community in some sort of mission statement, posted on the school's main web page or engraved onto a plaque in the school lobby so that all who visit can immediately see, "This is what we believe in," or perhaps, "If your child goes to school here, these are the educational ideals we will try to uphold."

Core values as articulated and agreed upon by a school's leadership can serve as a powerful foundation for LGBTQ-positive work that goes beyond mere safety. They can also be a basis from which to argue that such work is not only in keeping with the school's mission, it is essential to it. In less than five years, this Indiana school went from a place without a gay-straight alliance to one where administrators tout the GSA as one of the school's signature accomplishments and where LGBTQ issues are topics of frequent discussion among both students and staff. The successes in this conservative community illustrate how advocates who wish to move their schools from safety to inclusion should look first to existing schoolwide policies, goals, procedures, and philosophies. Many of these will support the argument for pro-LGBTQ programs simply because this work, at its core, is about helping all students achieve to their full potential.

AFTERWORD

Beyond "Better"

Envisioning the Ideal School
for LGBTQ Students

I BEGAN THIS BOOK with a reflection about the broader purpose of
public schooling in the United States and various perspectives on what
an ideal education might look like for the children and adolescents in
our nation's schools. Similarly, if we could imagine not just *better* schools
for LGBTQ students, but an *ideal* educational experience for them, as
well as for students growing up in LGBTQ-headed families, those with
LGBTQ siblings, or those who at some point in their lives will encounter LGBTQ people—essentially, every student—what would that school
experience look like, from preK through grade 12?

One way to envision such an ideal would be to imagine all of the elementary and secondary teachers, administrators, librarians, counselors,
district-level coordinators, volunteers, and consultants profiled in these
eight chapters working in one district. The brave educators interviewed
for this book are moving schools forward in a wide range of ways that
draw on their unique strengths. Some are working in communities where
changes are happening on multiple fronts. Others are working in rela-
tive isolation—if not a sole voice in their school, then one of only a few
advocating for an educational environment that is more than just safe
for their LGBTQ students. Some are working with the support of their
leadership; others are making a difference in spite of theirs. The notion
of all of them pooling their various strengths in one district is obviously
unrealistic—and undesirable from the perspective of the students who

would lose the valuable support and advocacy these educators provide in real schools all over the country. Nevertheless, the image that such an LGBTQ-inclusive "superdistrict" conjures is worth contemplating in that it raises two important questions: 1) Why would such an education for LGBTQ youth *not* be the norm? 2) How do we justify settling for anything less?

Based on the work profiled in the last eight chapters, an ideal school experience for LGBTQ youth might look something like the following.

THE SCHOOL BUILDING

As at Jericho Middle School on Long Island, it would be immediately apparent to any student, parent, educator, or community member who entered the building that LGBTQ individuals are not just "tolerated" but welcomed and embraced throughout every space of the school. This message would be clearly delivered in all the languages spoken by community members, and students' voices in communicating this message would be just as prominent as those of teachers and administrators.

Displays in the school library would show the wealth of LGBTQ-themed resources available in the school. Signs in the school's administrative offices, instead of sending messages of austerity and intimidation, would speak to the value of every student and their family—the signs might even be in rainbow colors, both literally and metaphorically, and illustrate the diversity of the community.

The discussion of LGBTQ-related topics would not be limited to spaces such as the GSA advisor's classroom or to dates such as National Coming Out Day or the Day of Silence but, as in Jericho, would be experienced by students as "just a part of what we do here."

THE CURRICULUM

As in the courses taught by Sara Barber-Just at Amherst High School in Massachusetts and Maggie Chesnut in New York City, students would have opportunities to learn about LGBTQ people and their contributions to society both as a discrete subject and in the context of other movements toward social justice. They would learn to make connections across various identity categories such as race, gender, sexual orientation, gender identity, and social class and examine the ways these categories do not neatly define people but instead interconnect, just as in the complex realities of their own lives.

As in Los Angeles, teachers would have clear and easy access to online resources that facilitate the teaching of lessons on issues related to LGBTQ identity. In addition, all textbooks would be inclusive of LGBTQ history and people, and no student would feel compelled to say, as the student quoted in chapter 1 did, that the curriculum they studied in school made it "easy to feel that I don't matter."

Education to combat biases about gender and sexual orientation would begin in (or before) elementary school, acknowledging that students are already forming ideas about these things in the early grades. Curriculum would be scaffolded in age-appropriate ways, and students would understand that their own and other students' families are valued, that their peers are worthy of respect regardless of any differences among them, and that hurtful words and actions can have a lasting impact.

SILENCE-FREE SCHOOLS

Students would feel free to discuss LGBTQ-related topics in classrooms, in hallways, in the cafeteria, and in all other spaces of the school building without negative repercussions from peers or adults. They would feel free to write about these topics for school assignments and to be out in school without fear that they will be ostracized or harassed. Like the students in Nixa, Missouri, they would have a strong sense of self-efficacy, understanding the power they have to communicate with school administrators, elected officials, and other decision makers to effect change. And, like the students in Park City, Utah, they would use social media and other technology not to cyberbully their peers but to extend the reach of their voices to LGBTQ students in other schools who need support.

As in Decatur's counseling sessions and Osceola's book discussion group, there would be multiple spaces in school, beyond the GSA, in which students could talk with their LGBTQ peers, whether it be about a book they can relate to or a challenge they are having with a love interest or their parents.

REAL INCLUSIVENESS

LGBTQ-inclusive programming in schools would be truly inclusive, across the LGBTQ spectrum and across differences in race, gender, religion, and socioeconomic status. LGBTQ-inclusive school programming would not be limited to middle-class suburbs in liberal enclaves of the Northeast and West Coast, but would also be provided to students in rural communities in the West, in the Bible Belt cities of the South, and in low-income neighborhoods in America's large cities. Gay-straight alliances and classes such as LGBTQ literature would not be viewed exclusively as a "white thing," a "girls' thing," or a "gay thing," but, as in Amherst, groups in which students across all categories of difference participate.

Transgender students, like those in Avon, Indiana, in Los Angeles, and at the Academy for Young Writers in Brooklyn, would have the right to attend school expressing gender in whatever way they choose—even if that means not expressing any gender at all. Students would learn about gender as a social construct, and the gender segregation affecting everything from gym classes to extracurricular activities would be, if not abolished, subject to thoughtful examination by students who have the intellectual tools to think critically about the dynamics of their school community.

TEACHERS AND MENTORS

Students would have both out LGBTQ teachers, like Sara Barber-Just, Maggie Chesnut, and Ken Jackson, and straight ally teachers, such as Bridget Brownell and Jackie Swindell. Teachers like Jeremy Charneco-Sullivan would not feel driven from their jobs because of homophobia and transphobia; instead, school administrations would actively recruit a diversity of teachers, including LGBTQ teachers, to serve as mentors and role models for their students, recognizing that the ability to imagine future "possible selves" is an important developmental need for adolescents.

In addition, teachers would be in ongoing dialogue about ways to serve as effective resources to LGBTQ students and incorporate LGBTQ-related topics into curriculum. Teachers would have access to classes about LGBTQ issues as well as one-on-one coaching geared to integrating LGBTQ issues into various subject areas, like that provided by Elisa Waters in Jericho. In addition to the support of their teachers, students would benefit from mentorship and guidance from adults in the community, like Adam Chang and Josephine Chang at Farrington High School in Honolulu. Parents and other family members would be involved in commemorations that celebrate LGBTQ identities at school, just as they are for sports and other extracurricular activities, and students would feel supported by counselors and other school staff in issues associated with coming out to family members and friends.

LEADERSHIP

Like Principal Don Gately in Jericho, school leaders would be involved in the lives of LGBTQ students, attending GSA meetings and advocating for their rights both to the school community and to their professional colleagues. These leaders would know when to lead and when to follow—willing to learn from LGBTQ students and teachers but also willing to defend their rights to parents or other community members who might oppose LGBTQ-friendly programming.

POLICY

Policies at the local, state, and federal levels would support LGBTQ students' right to attend school free from discrimination and with their identities honored and represented. The "no homo promo" laws that still exist in eight states and that lead teachers to censor themselves from discussing LGBTQ issues in the classroom would be abolished. Instead of laws in less than half of the states, there would be federal legislation that prohibited discrimination in public schools on the basis of sexual orientation, gender, and gender identity across the country. As in Los Angeles, policies would outline clearly and unambiguously for administrators, teachers, and other school staff their responsibilities under the law in real-world classroom and school scenarios. Protected by such policies, teachers would feel free to honor their students' gender identities and sexual orientations without fear of censure.

To some readers, the "ideal" school system I have depicted here—based on an amalgamation of the work profiled throughout this book—may sound utopian. For most readers, I hope that by now its necessity is obvious. In any case, it is a long way from being realized for many students in the United States. Despite all the gains of the safe schools movement and the tremendous difference this work has made, about one in four LGBTQ youth still attempts suicide at some point in their adolescence.[1] Fewer than one in five have the opportunity to study LGBTQ issues in any of their classes at school, and more than half experience harassment based on their gender identity or sexual orientation.[2] These statistics were even worse twenty years ago, but even if conditions have improved, clearly they haven't improved enough. And, as some of the evidence presented in this book suggests, on some fronts and in some schools, they seem hardly to have improved at all.

Arguing for all students to be safe at school was the right strategy in the political climate of the late twentieth century, when LGBTQ individuals—both in law and in public opinion—were viewed as "less than" their straight counterparts. Although we may still be a long way from full LGBTQ inclusion in American society, there are hopeful signs that the current generation of LGBTQ youth can grow up in a different world, where instead of being silenced they will have many opportunities to be leaders. We can hear such a future in the words of the openly LGBTQ students at Brooklyn's Academy for Young Writers, who are inspiring younger students to join the GSA and be proud of their identities. We also can hear it in the voices of the students in Nixa, Missouri, and Park City, Utah, who are meeting with elected officials in their state capitols and advocating for change. The educators who support these students are fostering qualities such as self-efficacy, empowerment, and pride among their LGBTQ students, and the fact that some are doing it in the face of intense political and religious opposition makes clear that achieving to a standard beyond "safe" is possible anywhere.

APPENDIX A

Artifacts of Practice

THE ARTIFACTS OF PRACTICE in this appendix include a course syllabus, classroom handouts, GSA and counseling materials, and other resources that illustrate the range of work profiled in this book. All are reprinted here with the permission of the educators or institutions that provided them and are included as examples of work that can be adapted for a variety of educational settings.

EXHIBIT 1.1 Syllabus for Sara Barber-Just's Course "LGBTQ Literature" at Amherst (MA) High School

---

LGBTQ (LESBIAN, GAY, BISEXUAL, TRANSGENDER, QUEER/QUESTIONING) LITERATURE

Ms. Barber-Just

Students in public schools have been reading literary classics by LGBTQ authors for more than a century; however, these authors' lives are often concealed rather than rightfully explored. This course closely examines the struggles and triumphs of these artists—as well as the historical periods during which they wrote—allowing readers to more deeply analyze their diverse literary contributions. LGBTQ Literature is split into five major sections, moving in chronological order from the early 1900s to the present day. Class readings include works written by lesbian, gay, bisexual, transgender, and queer authors during eras of severe legal and social oppression; conformity and self-loathing; anger, activism, and radicalism; and, finally, pride and acceptance. The course focuses on renowned modern

EXHIBIT 1.1   *continued*

and contemporary American authors such as Willa Cather, James Baldwin, Rita Mae Brown, and Michael Cunningham. Students working at the AP level will also read two additional texts from any of the following writers: Oscar Wilde, Isabel Miller, Charles Rice-Gonzalez, Shyam Selvadurai, Alice Walker, Leslie Feinberg, Jeffrey Eugenides, Judith Frank, Colm Tóibín, and more. Each unit includes a combination of critical essays, articles, poetry, short story, and/or film, providing a rich cultural and historical context for the featured literature. You will no doubt leave this class with a better understanding of LGBTQ people, their unique and vibrant culture and literature, and their search for inclusion and representation.

Syllabus:

First 2–3 weeks: The Early 1900s–1930s

   A Lost Lady, by Willa Cather

   LGBTQ subtext in literature and media analysis

   The Celluloid Closet

Next 3 weeks: The 1950s

   Giovanni's Room, by James Baldwin

   Gay identity development models

   The biology of gender and sexuality

Next 3 weeks: The 1970s and '80s

   Rubyfruit Jungle, by Rita Mae Brown

   "A Letter to Harvey Milk," by Leslea Newman

   "Generation LGBTQIA," *New York Times*

   Essays and poetry

Next 3 weeks: The 1990s

   The Hours, by Michael Cunningham

   Excerpts from *Mrs. Dalloway*, by Virginia Woolf

Last 2 weeks: Transgender/genderqueer articles, film, speakers

EXHIBIT 1.1   *continued*

HONORS/AP PROJECTS

11th and 12th grade literature students may complete one independent project (in one class) for honors credit and two independent projects (over two courses) for AP credit (one classical, one contemporary). Each project requires reading at least two additional novels and taking an AP essay test at both the midterm and the last two weeks of the term. Honors and AP projects are worth 20% of a student's overall course grade. Juniors wishing to change from the Honors or AP designation to a College Prep designation MUST complete the drop by the midterm; seniors must make any changes in English courses by the midterm of the first trimester of their senior year.

**EXHIBIT 1.2   Sample assignment from Sara Barber-Just's course
"LGBTQ Literature" at Amherst (MA) High School**

LGBTQ Notions
Personal Awareness Assignment

Due: _____

As a class, we watched the film *The Celluloid Closet*, examining the role of LGBTQ people in films over the past 100 years. Then, we generated a list of LGBTQ stereotypes as a class.

Using your notes from the film *and* our class discussion, go about your daily life and record some of the images and ideas you encounter about LGBTQ people. Increase your awareness. Open your eyes and mind.

You must collect FOUR observations and then write ONE paragraph each about EACH observation. Be sure to include a description of the observation in detail *and* a determination about whether this observation is positive or negative and WHY. Also, provide visuals (this is required) from a magazine, online, links to songs, etc.

When your project is complete, you will have:

- written four paragraphs about four different images/events/observations. These will be typed and double-spaced (about two pages total).
- sent an email to me with links to at least two of your ideas. You may be sending me a film trailer, a YouTube video, a link to a song/music video, a clip of a television show, a link to a *New York Times* article, or a link to an article in *Out* magazine or *The Advocate*.

DON'T PANIC! You will most likely find more than four LGBTQ notions within this time period.

Some suggestions:

- Look for representation of LGBTQ people in the media: television, advertising, newspapers, cartoons, movies, etc.
- Look at employment patterns. Where do you see LGBTQ people in positions of power? Where are they disenfranchised or under-represented?

EXHIBIT 1.2 *continued*

- Look at housing patterns. Where do LGBTQ people live? Where do fewer LGBTQ people live openly?
- Read a gay newspaper/magazine (*Out, The Advocate, Curve, Bay Windows*), then a mainstream one, and compare the ads/ideas. (You can find these magazines at libraries, bookstores, and online.)
- Happenings/treatment at ARHS.
- Happenings in your neighborhood.
- What your friends are saying/doing.

Overall: think consciously about what you may be subconsciously learning about LGBTQ people!

EXHIBIT 2.1 **Why Our Middle School Has a Gay-Straight Alliance**

Donald F. Gately, EdD

Donald Gately, principal of Jericho Middle School, posts a regular blog linked to the school's website (https://dfgately.wordpress.com). He uses the blog to discuss issues of concern to the Jericho community and share his experiences working as a school administrator with colleagues in other schools. Some of his blog posts are more personal (he recently wrote about his efforts to learn Spanish) as a way to help people in the Jericho community get to know him better.

By far the most widely viewed posting in the history of Gately's blog has been the following piece, presented in question-and-answer format to reflect the kinds of questions and comments Gately says he has received about the school's GSA from parents, community members, and his administrative colleagues in other schools. The blog post received an estimated 550 views in its first day online, attesting to the number of educators who want to do more to help middle school students navigate LGBTQ issues but don't know where to begin.

Last week, Jericho Middle School hosted a forum on lesbian, gay, bisexual, and transgender (LGBT) issues in education. The forum was organized by one of our teachers, Elisa Waters, along with her colleagues and students as well as the Nassau County Anti-Bias Consortium. Over 150 educators heard presentations by experts from our field on topics related to LGBT issues. The keynote speaker, Eliza Byard, is the executive director of the Gay, Lesbian and Straight Education Network (GLSEN). She is a nationally known civil rights leader who has been outspoken in support of legislation and other efforts to protect the rights of LGBT individuals. She spoke alongside President Obama at the 50th anniversary of the Civil Rights March on Washington, which was recently held at the Lincoln Memorial.

EXHIBIT 2.1   *continued*

It was a privilege to host this event, and I am proud that we have a Gay-Straight Alliance (GSA) Club for students at Jericho Middle School. We have had a club here for over 10 years. We owe its success mainly to the leadership of Elisa, who has been a groundbreaking educator on Long Island in bringing these issues to the forefront of people's attention. Since this event, I have been thinking about the many conversations I have had over the last 10 years about the GSA and I thought I would put some of these ideas into writing to offer guidance to other educators who are thinking about starting a club in their school, or to educators or individuals who feel that the middle school is not the right place for a GSA club. I have organized these thoughts in the form of Frequently Asked Questions.

Aren't middle school kids too young for this?

When I was in 6th grade, I had my first crush on a girl. Her name was Joanne and she sat next to me in class. She was all I thought about. I couldn't concentrate because all I wanted to do was steal glances at Joanne. Every time I raised my hand to answer a question, I wondered what Joanne thought about what I said. I thought about Joanne at the expense of everything else, like homework, and spelling tests and remembering to walk the dog. It might have helped if I spoke to an adult about this, like a parent or a teacher, but I was too embarrassed. If I had talked to a grown-up, they certainly would have told me that what I was experiencing was completely normal. They could have reassured me that I was going to be okay; eventually I would be able to concentrate on social studies again. But I didn't discuss my feelings with any adults. I kept them to myself.

Has this ever happened to you? How old were you when you developed your first crush? Did you tell anybody? What was the reaction you received? What would you want the reaction to be if it was your child? How about our students? When do you think they begin to realize who they are attracted to?

EXHIBIT 2.1   *continued*

The fact is, middle school is the time when individuals become aware of these kinds of attractions. Shouldn't children who are gay feel supported and normal, just like heterosexual children? I believe that EVERY child should feel accepted in school, should feel like they are normal and OK; that school is a place where they belong. I know that children learn better under these conditions. That's an important reason a school should have a GSA. So that all students feel like they are accepted and so that kids learn to accept others.

But Don, adolescents haven't really figured this out for themselves yet.

Maybe, but shouldn't they be supported and made to feel good about themselves while they do figure it out?

But Don, why encourage it?

Science and the law are pretty clear on this point: Being gay is not a "choice"; it's part of what makes us who we are. The American Psychiatric Association has condemned "psychiatric treatment" such as reparative or conversion therapy, which is based upon the assumption that homosexuality is a disorder and that a patient should change his/her sexual orientation. Just two weeks ago a federal judge in New Jersey upheld a law barring therapists from trying to turn gay youth straight. Having a GSA, or LGBT programs, isn't going to "make anybody gay."

But this club is about sex. I don't think my child even knows about sex yet . . . I don't want him/her learning about this in school.

Firstly, sex isn't discussed at middle school GSA meetings. It just isn't.

Secondly, being gay and gay marriage are no more about sex than being heterosexual and heterosexual marriage are. It's about who you want to love and spend your life with. It's a natural, human impulse to want to share your life with somebody who you think is special. My wife is my best friend. We do all kinds of fun things together. I want to be with her all the time. When something good or bad in my life happens,

EXHIBIT 2.1 *continued*

she's the first person I want to talk to about it. We are each other's biggest cheerleaders and teachers. She is the person I count on and she knows she can count on me. Doesn't everybody deserve this? And what about students? If a kid at the middle school has gay parents or gay uncles or aunts, shouldn't they feel like they can talk about their families in the same way the children of heterosexual kids do? Should they be embarrassed about this or feel it's some kind of secret?

Why do other kids attend the GSA? Isn't it for gay kids?

Don't forget, the "S" and the "A" in GSA stand for "straight allies." When I was a student at Queens College I noticed a plaque dedicated to Andrew Goodman, who was one of the students who traveled to Mississippi to march for civil rights in the 1960s. He was killed along with two other men by the Ku Klux Klan because of their efforts to win equality and civil rights for African-Americans. Andrew Goodman was white. I am proud that I attended the same college as Andrew Goodman. The fact is, no civil rights movement has ever succeeded without the support of members of the majority. This is the main focus of our bully prevention program. We encourage students to be positive bystanders, to stand up for those who are being bullied. That's what it says on our T-shirts, "We Don't Stand By—We Stand Up." Frankly, at a GSA meeting, I have no idea who is gay and who isn't. Students come together to learn about each other and how to be accepting of all people, including LGBT people. Also, there is a significant and growing body of research that demonstrates that schools that have GSAs are safer and more bully-free for all kids, not just gay students.

What about religious objections to the gay lifestyle?

I'm Catholic. I went to Catholic school for nearly 16 years. No one ever taught me to make anybody feel bad about themselves. I wasn't taught to exclude people or deprive anyone of their rights because they are gay. There's nothing anti-Catholic about a Gay-Straight Alliance. As far as I know, most religions of the world are committed to helping others

EXHIBIT 2.1 *continued*

and making the world a better place. Besides, public schools can neither endorse nor discriminate against anyone's religious beliefs; I cannot think of a valid religious objection to having a Gay-Straight Alliance in our school.

But when kids say, "That's so gay," it's not a biased remark; they just mean, "That's stupid."

That's not okay. We all have many identities: teacher, Italian, parent, coach, Catholic, stamp collector, Jew, basketball player, cop, attorney, Muslim, cook . . . Everyone is entitled to be proud of their various identities and be free from harassment because of these. Being gay is part of a person's identity; why should it be acceptable for anyone to use this as a pejorative? I'm of Irish descent. I'm proud of this. If kids said, "That's so Irish" whenever they thought something was stupid, that would make me angry.

Why do we need a GSA? Aren't we accepting enough?

I wish we didn't need a GSA. I wish that kids didn't call each other "faggot" and "gay" as the put-down of choice in middle school. But they do. I wish young gay adults didn't commit suicide because they feel like they are not normal or because they are rejected or harassed by their peers. But they do. I hope one day that the Gay-Straight Alliance is an anachronism, an interesting artifact from an earlier, less tolerant period in history. Meanwhile, I strongly believe we need a Gay-Straight Alliance here and at every other middle school in our country.

CONCLUSION

It is important for me to note that I did not come to the ideas I have expressed in this post overnight. I was not as open in my views about these issues as I am now. I have come to a better understanding of the issues surrounding gay, lesbian, bisexual, and transgender individuals through many conversations I have had with enlightened people who

EXHIBIT 2.1 *continued*

have shared with me their stories. I have also come to a greater understanding as I have spent time in a leadership position defending this club over the eight years I have been principal. The questions I addressed above come from conversations I've had with actual parents, educators, and other people who have expressed to me their reservations about the Gay-Straight Alliance.

Many teachers and administrators attended the LGBTeach forum because they were looking for insights and guidance as to how to bring these efforts into their own schools throughout Long Island. Just as I have evolved in my thinking over the past many years, I would invite you to do the same. If I can do it, you can do it. And so can the people in your community. I have found the best way to overcome resistance is through face-to-face dialogue. It might sound trite, but the more we get to know each other the more we learn to accept each other. Jericho is a special community and we have the benefit of an extremely supportive board of education and the courageous leadership of our superintendent, Hank Grishman. I am privileged to be the principal of a remarkable school with amazing teachers who are doing exciting work in many areas, including teaching about LGBT rights and acceptance. We would be more than happy to work with anyone to bring a Gay-Straight Alliance Club to their school . . . just give us a call.

EXHIBIT 4.1   Farrington High School GSA 2014–2015 calendar of events

During the 2014–2015 school year, members of the Farrington High School GSA participated in a wide variety of activities that were illustrative of the range of LGBTQ-positive experiences students can have as part of these groups. Their annual agenda included guest speakers, lessons on LGBTQ-related topics such as the Kinsey scale and Harvey Milk High School in New York City, a trivia game, commemorations of events such as National Coming Out Day, and a field trip to hear Farrington alum and prominent transgender writer and activist Janet Mock on the University of Hawaii campus. Following is the calendar of events maintained by advisors Alison Colby and Gwen Murakami for the 2014–2015 school year.

FARRINGTON GSA MEETINGS 2014–15

Co-advisors: Alison Colby, Gwen Murakami

Month	Date	Advisor/ Mentor	Lesson	Notes/Icebreakers
July	23	Alison/Gwen	Sign-Ups	Schedule Pick-Up
August	1	Alison/Gwen	What is the GSA?	Freshman Assembly
	21–22	Alison	Club Rush Days	
	22	Alison/Gwen	Introductions, Orientation, Brainstorming the year	First meeting
	29	Alison/Gwen	LGBT terminology; Kinsey scale posters	
September	5	Gwen	LGBT Myths and Facts	Students presenting
	19	Adam	Gender spectrum	
	26	Alison/Gwen	LGBT Timeline	

EXHIBIT 4.1 *continued*

Month	Date	Advisor/ Mentor	Lesson	Notes/Icebreakers
October	3	Jo	LGBT History Month	Term 1 ends
	13–17	Alison/Gwen	Ally Week art project	Ribbon and pen rainbow lei
	17	Guest speaker	Personal Story	Transgender female-to-male speaker
	24	Alison/Gwen	Planning, Term 2	
	28	Alison/Gwen	Mix It Up Day	Speak out, GSA booth
	31	Alison/Gwen	Masks Activity and games	Academic Challenge, lunch time bento!
November	14	Adam	LGBT Trivia Game	
	21	Adam	Harvey Milk HS debate	
December	1–2	Alison/Gwen	Community Service	FACF newsletter folding
	5	Guest speaker	Community outreach project	Yearbook picture-taking
	12	Alison/Gwen	Christmas Celebration	Term 2 ends
January	16	Alison/Gwen	Re-Group: review, reconnect, plan	
	19	Alison	Martin Luther King, Jr. Parade	GSA Hawaii, GLSEN
	20–23	Alison/Gwen	No Name-Calling Week	Flyers, bulletin, kindness count
	23	Alison/Gwen	StoryCorps stories, writing project	
	30	Alison/Gwen	Field Trip	Community Service

EXHIBIT 4.1   *continued*

Month	Date	Advisor/ Mentor	Lesson	Notes/Icebreakers
February	6	Alison/Gwen	Video screenings	Makino Chaya!— Academic Challenge
	13	Guest speaker	Relationship violence	
	20	Alison/Gwen	Prepare for Rainbow Popcorn! event	
March	6	Alison/Gwen	Rainbow Popcorn!	
	13	Alison/Gwen	Videotaping, Trivia Game 2	Term 3 ends
	20	Gwen	Community Service Field Trip: Ho'oulu 'Aina	Spring Break
	27	Guest speaker	Prep for Day of Silence: button-making	
April	10	Alison/Gwen	Prep for Janet's talk; book excerpts	
	16	Alison/Gwen	Janet Mock at UH!	Reception, Speaking, Book Sign
	17	Alison/Gwen	DOS/Breaking the Silence	Academic Challenge Lunch time bento!
	24	Guest speaker	Personal Story	Gay physician
May	1	Alison/Gwen	LGBT terminology game; writing project, flyers	May Day
	15	Alison/Gwen	Evaluation, Planning for Next Year	
	22	Alison/Gwen	Celebration!	Last meeting

Regular meetings are held after school at the Teen Center, J278, on Fridays, from about 3:10 to 4:00 pm, followed by informal social time. School and community activities will be built into the calendar as the year progresses.

EXHIBIT 5.1   Los Angeles Unified School District policy bulletin

TITLE: Transgender Students—Ensuring Equity and Nondiscrimination
NUMBER: BUL-6224.0
ISSUER: David Holmquist, General Counsel Office of General Counsel
DATE: February 7, 2014

PURPOSE:
The Los Angeles Unified School District (District) is committed to providing a safe and supportive learning environment for all students and to ensuring that every student shall have equal access to the District's educational programs and activities. Additionally, District policy requires that all schools and all personnel promote acceptance and respect among students and staff.

This policy reflects the reality that transgender and gender nonconforming students are enrolled in the District. Its purpose is to advise District staff regarding issues relating to transgender students in order to create and maintain a safe learning environment for all students. The guidelines provided in this Bulletin do not anticipate every situation that might occur with respect to transgender students. The needs of each transgender student are unique. This policy should be interpreted consistent with the goals of reducing stigmatization and ensuring the integration of transgender students in educational programs and activities.

California Education Code §210.7 states that "gender means sex," and includes a person's gender identity and gender-related appearance and behavior whether or not stereotypically associated with the person's assigned sex at birth.

California Education Code §220 and District policy require that all educational programs and activities should be conducted without discrimination based on actual or perceived sex, sexual orientation, or gender identity and expression.

California Education Code §201 provides that public schools have an affirmative obligation to combat sexism and other forms of bias, and a responsibility to provide an equal educational opportunity to all students.

Title IX of the Education Amendments of 1972 states, "No person . . . shall, on the basis of sex, be excluded from participation in, be denied

EXHIBIT 5.1   *continued*

the benefits of, or be subjected to discrimination under any education program or activity receiving federal financial assistance."

This Bulletin provides guidelines to ensure protection, respectful treatment, and equal access to educational programs and activities for transgender students.

MAJOR CHANGES: This Bulletin replaces REF-1557.1, "Transgender and Gender Variant Students—Ensuring Equity and Nondiscrimination," dated September 9, 2011, issued by the Office of General Counsel. It provides updated information and guidance to schools regarding issues related to transgender students.

INSTRUCTIONS: I. Definitions—The following definitions are not meant to label, but are intended as functional descriptors:

A. Gender: a person's actual sex or perceived sex, and includes a person's perceived identity, appearance, or behavior, whether or not that identity, appearance, or behavior is different from that traditionally associated with a person's sex at birth [Title 5, California Code of Regulations, §4910(k)].

B. Gender Identity: a person's internal, deeply rooted identification as female, male, or a non-binary understanding of gender, regardless of one's assigned sex at birth. The responsibility for determining an individual's gender identity rests with the individual.

C. Gender Expression: A person's gender-related appearance and behavior whether or not stereotypically associated with the person's assigned sex at birth. Students who adopt a presentation that varies from the stereotypic gender expectations sometimes may describe themselves as gender nonconforming, gender queer, or gender fluid.

D. Gender Nonconforming: Displaying a gender identity or expression that may differ from those typically associated with one's sex assigned

EXHIBIT 5.1 *continued*

at birth. A person's gender expression may differ from stereotypical expectations about how females and males are "supposed to" look or act. Gender nonconforming is not synonymous with transgender; not all gender-nonconforming students identify as transgender.

E. Transgender: A person whose gender identity differs from their gender assigned at birth, and whose gender expression consistently varies from stereotypical expectations and norms. A transgender person desires to live persistently by a gender that differs from that which was assigned at birth.

F. Transition: Each transgender person has a unique process in which they go from living and identifying as one gender to living and identifying as another. Gender transition can occur at any age. It begins internally then expands to external expression. This can include social, medical, and/or a legal transition.

G. LGBTQ: An acronym that stands for "lesbian, gay, bisexual, transgender, and queer/questioning." Questioning incorporates those who are uncertain or fluid about their sexual orientation and/or gender identity.

H. Sex: The biological condition or quality of being female or male.

I. Sexual Orientation: A person's emotional and sexual attraction to another person based on the gender of the other person. Common terms used to describe sexual orientation include, but are not limited to, heterosexual, lesbian, gay, and bisexual. Sexual orientation and gender identity are different.

II. Guidelines
The school shall accept the gender identity that each student asserts. There is no medical or mental health diagnosis or treatment threshold that students must meet in order to have their gender identity recognized and respected. The assertion may be evidenced by an expressed desire

EXHIBIT 5.1 *continued*

to be consistently recognized by their gender identity. Students ready to socially transition may initiate a process to change their name, pronoun, attire, and access to preferred activities and facilities. Each student has a unique process for transitioning. The school shall customize support to optimize each student's integration.

A. Privacy and Confidentiality

1. All persons, including students, have a right to privacy. This includes keeping a student's actual or perceived gender identity and expression private. Such private information shall be shared only on a need-to-know basis.

2. Students have the right to openly discuss and express their gender identity and expression, and to decide when, with whom, and how much information to share.

3. District and school personnel may encounter situations where transgender students have not disclosed their transgender status. School personnel must be mindful of the confidentiality and privacy rights of students when communicating with others, so as to not reveal, imply, or refer to a student's gender identity or expression.

4. To ensure confidentiality when discussing a particular concern such as conduct, discipline, grades, attendance, or health, school personnel's focus should be specifically school-related and not on the student's gender identity or expression.

B. Official Records

1. The District is required to maintain in perpetuity mandatory permanent pupil records ("official records") which include the legal name of the student and the student's gender as indicated on official government issued documents such as birth certificates, passports and identification cards/permits. The official records may include but are not limited to progress and grade reports,

EXHIBIT 5.1 *continued*

transcripts, assessment data, health records, discipline records, Individualized Education Programs (IEP), Section 504 Plans, and the cumulative card and file (folder).

2. The District will change a student's name and gender on official records when the name of the student is changed by the appropriate court action, such as by a change of name proceedings. The new name is the official legal name of the student for all purposes, including school registration. Upon the submission of proper evidence of the court order, the student's official name and gender in all school records shall be changed to reflect the legal name change.

C. Unofficial Records

1. The District shall permit a student to use a preferred name and gender on unofficial records. The unofficial records may include but are not limited to identification badges, classroom and homeroom rosters, certificates, programs, announcements, office summons and communications, team and academic rosters, diplomas, newspapers, newsletters, yearbooks, and other site-generated unofficial records. The preferred name shall also appear on the student's cumulative folder (official record) as "Also Known As" (AKA).

2. The District shall input the student's preferred name and gender in the appropriate fields of the District's electronic data system to indicate how the student's name and gender will appear on unofficial records.

3. The District shall permit a student or parent/legal guardian to request a change of name and/or gender so that a student may be registered in school under a name and gender that corresponds with the student's gender identity without obtaining a court order or without changing the student's official records (see "Names of Pupils for Purposes of School Records," BUL-5703.1,

EXHIBIT 5.1   *continued*

---

dated February 27, 2012, issued by the Office of Data and Accountability).

4. After the school receives and verifies the contents of the completed form, the school shall change the name and/or gender of the student in the District's electronic data system and enter the preferred name as AKA in the cumulative folder. In the cumulative folder and registration card, name and gender should be cross-referenced.

D. Names/Pronouns

1. Students shall be addressed by the name and pronoun that corresponds to their gender identity asserted at school without obtaining a court order, changing their official records or obtaining parent/legal guardian permission.

2. Students shall be known by their name and gender of identity. However, there may be situations (e.g., communications with the family, official state or federal records, and assessment data) where it may be necessary and recommended for staff to be informed of the student's legal name and gender. In these situations, staff should prioritize the safety, confidentiality, and respect of the student in a manner that affirms the law.

3. If school personnel are unsure how a student wants to be addressed in communications to the home or in conferences with parents/legal guardians, they may privately ask the student. For communications with a student's parent/legal guardian, school personnel should refer to this policy's prior section on "Privacy and Confidentiality."

4. Every effort should be made to use the preferred names and pronouns consistent with a student's gender identity. While inadvertent slips or honest mistakes may occur, the intentional and persistent refusal to respect a student's gender identity is a violation of District policy.

EXHIBIT 5.1   *continued*

E. Restroom Accessibility

1. Schools may maintain separate restroom facilities for male and female students. Students shall have access to restrooms that correspond to their gender identity asserted at school.
2. If a student desires increased privacy, regardless of the underlying reason, the administrator shall make every effort to provide the student with reasonable access to an alternative restroom such as a single-stall restroom or the health office restroom. The use of a restroom should be determined by the student's choice; no student shall be compelled to use an alternative restroom.
3. Administrators may take steps to designate single stall "gender neutral" restrooms on their campus.

F. Locker Room Accessibility

1. Schools may maintain separate locker room facilities for male and female students. Students shall have access to the locker room facility that corresponds to their gender identity asserted at school.
2. If there is a request for increased privacy, *any* student shall be provided access to a reasonable accommodation such as:

   a.   Assignment of a student locker in near proximity to the coaches' office or a supportive peer group.

   b.   Use of a private area within the public area of the locker room facility (e.g., nearby restroom stall with a door or an area separated by a curtain).

   c.   Use of a nearby private area (e.g., nearby restroom or a health office restroom).

   d.   A separate changing schedule.

G. Sports, Athletics, and Physical Education

1. Physical education classes are typically co-gender. In the event that the classes or activities are sex-segregated, transgender

EXHIBIT 5.1   *continued*

students shall participate in physical education by their gender identity asserted at school.

2. When conducting physical education classes and fitness evaluations, the teacher will address and evaluate the student by their gender of identity. Performance on the state physical fitness test (Fitnessgram) is evaluated by the State of California in accordance with the sex reported on the student's initial enrollment, even when the student identifies as transgender. In these events, the physical education teacher shall make every effort to maintain confidentiality of student information.

3. Participation in competitive athletics, intramural sports, athletic teams, competitions, and contact sports shall be facilitated in a manner consistent with the student's gender identity asserted at school and in accordance with the California Interscholastic Federation bylaws (Gender Identity Participation, 300.D, page 56).

H. School Activities and Programs

Students have the right to equitable access to activities and programs in their school. Students may not be excluded from participation in, be denied the benefits of, or be subjected to harassment or other forms of discrimination on the basis of gender identity in any program or activity. These activities and programs may include but are not limited to cheer class, homecoming, prom, spirit day, celebrations, assemblies, acknowledgments, after school activities/programs, and all extra-curricular activities.

I. Course Accessibility and Instruction

Students have the right to equitable learning opportunities in their school. Students shall not be required to take and/or be denied enrollment in a course on the basis of their gender identity in any educational and academic program.

EXHIBIT 5.1   *continued*

J. Dress Codes/School Uniform Policies

1. A school's dress code and school uniform policy shall be gender-neutral. Schools cannot enforce specific attire based on gender.
2. Students have the right to dress in accordance with their gender identity within the parameters of the dress code, as it relates to the school uniform or safety issues (e.g., prohibiting attire that promotes drugs or violence, or is gang-affiliated).

K. Student Safety

1. School staff must ensure that students are provided with a safe school environment that is free of discrimination, harassment, bullying, and/or intimidation.
2. School staff and families should work together to resolve complaints alleging discrimination, harassment, bullying, and/or intimidation based on a student's actual or perceived gender identity or expression. Complaints of this nature are to be handled in the same manner as other complaints. Consideration should be given as to whether a Sexual Harassment investigation is warranted. [See the "Related Resources" and the "Assistance" sections of this Bulletin and BUL-3349.0, Sexual Harassment Policy (Student-to-Student, Adult-to-Student, and Student-to-Adult, dated November 29, 2006, issued by the Office of General Counsel).]
3. School staff shall take all reported incidents of bullying seriously and take appropriate measures to ensure that the bullying stops. [See BUL-5212.1 *Bullying and Hazing Policy (Student-to-Student and Student-to-Adult)*, dated September 17, 2012, issued by the Office of the Superintendent].
4. School administration shall respond immediately to incidents of discrimination, harassment, bullying, and/or intimidation by taking actions that include, but are not limited to the following: a) intervening to stop the behavior; b) investigating and documenting

EXHIBIT 5.1   *continued*

the incident; c) determining and enforcing appropriate corrective actions; and d) monitoring to ensure that the behavior does not reoccur.

5. School staff should take all reasonable steps to ensure safety and access for transgender and gender-nonconforming students at their school. School staff shall support students' rights to assert their gender identity and expression.

6. Students shall not be disciplined solely on the basis of their actual or perceived gender identity or expression.

7. Students shall be informed that they have the responsibility to report situations/incidents of discrimination, harassment, bullying, and/or intimidation to the designated site administrator or Title IX/Bullying Complaint Manager in cases where they may be a target or witness.

8. Students shall be informed of their role in ensuring a school environment that is free from discrimination, harassment, bullying, and/or intimidation. Students should consider how others may perceive or be affected by their actions and words.

EXHIBIT 6.1   Decatur High School group information prescreening form

Ken Jackson and other members of the counseling staff at Decatur (GA) High School follow a series of steps before a student joins the LGBTQ counseling group to ensure that such a fit would be appropriate both for them and for the other members of the group. The steps consist of the following:

1. A needs assessment (based on a beginning-of-the-year general survey) or other self-referral
2. Completion of the "Group Information Pre-Screening Form"
3. An individual prescreen interview to assess:
   - identity appropriate for the group;
   - understanding of confidentiality requirements and limitations;
   - social skills appropriate for work in a group setting;
   - age, grade;
   - identity development stage; and
   - assent of student.

The Group Information Pre-Screening Form (step 2) used by counselors at Decatur High School is presented on the following pages.

EXHIBIT 6.1   *continued*

GROUP INFORMATION PRE-SCREENING FORM

Name _____   Date _____

Grade Level _____

Please answer the following as you feel comfortable. You may leave one blank if you prefer.

Gender _____   Race _____

I identify as (circle all that apply):

- Gay
- Lesbian
- Bisexual
- Transgender
- Queer
- Questioning
- Straight
- Other _____

Answer the following questions only if you put anything but "straight" on the above.

How long have you thought that you might be non-straight (LGBTQ)?

_____

Are you "out" (open about being non-straight) to the following? (Circle all that apply.) Feel free to clarify if necessary.

- A friend or closest friends
- All my friends
- All people my age in general
- Only to people who ask me

EXHIBIT 6.1 *continued*

- My parents/guardians
- My extended family
- My church
- Other LGBTQ people
- List other groups of people

_____

If you are "out" to any of the above, how long have you been out?

- A friend or closest friends   _____
- All my friends   _____
- All people my age in general   _____
- Only to people who ask me   _____
- My parents/guardians   _____
- My extended family   _____
- My church   _____
- Other LGBTQ people   _____
- Others

_____

How comfortable are you in being out?

1	2	3	4	5

Not at all   Almost all the time

Explain: _____

_____

_____

How good do you feel most of the time about who you are?

1	2	3	4	5

Terrible   Great

EXHIBIT 6.1 *continued*

What are some of the primary stressors or areas of concern in your life right now?

_____

_____

_____

_____

_____

_____

_____

Why do you want to be in a group counseling situation?

_____

_____

_____

_____

_____

What else do you want me to know?

_____

_____

_____

_____

_____

EXHIBIT 7.1 **Responding to some concerns about being LGBT-inclusive** (from *Welcoming Schools: An Inclusive Approach to Addressing Family Diversity, Gender Stereotyping, and Name-Calling in K–5 Learning Environments*)

When you try to be inclusive of lesbian, gay, bisexual, and transgender people and topics, questions and concerns may arise in conversations with parents, guardians, administrators or school boards. This section provides ideas on how to discuss concerns or questions.

While conversations about race, ethnicity, class and religion remain difficult for many people, our society generally shares the value of respect—or at least tolerance—for people who are of a different religious, racial, cultural or ethnic background than our own. We can largely agree that certain race-based or religious-based slurs are unacceptable, and we expect educators and all school related personnel to intervene when they see or hear name-calling or harassment based on characteristics associated with these categories.

However, anti-LGBT attitudes or behavior are often tolerated, and many students still "get away" with using slurs or words that are very hurtful to LGBT people and their families. Because LGBT people and topics are often not included in antibias work or conversations about diversity, it may be that educators and parents/guardians in your school community have less knowledge of or comfort with these conversations.

It is always helpful to emphasize your values instead of dwelling on the fears. Move the conversation from focusing on the myths and stereotypes about lesbian, gay, bisexual and transgender people and families to emphasizing what this work is really about—supporting all students. If conversations are framed by myths and stereotypes, the resulting dialogue is more likely to linger on negativity and fear rather than focusing on positive aspects of welcoming schools.

Listen carefully to the concerns that are expressed. This will help you find points of agreement. For example, we all share values of family and respect. What follows are some examples of specific language that might be helpful.

EXHIBIT 7.1   *continued*

WE ARE TALKING ABOUT FAMILY.

Families of all kinds are essential to students' well-being. When any parents or guardians are discussed, whether they are heterosexual, gay, adoptive, kinship, single or married, educators are simply discussing family.

- Roberto is talking about his family when he talks about visiting his grandparents with his two moms and younger brother, just as Sasha is talking about her family when she describes her vacation with her mommy, daddy, and sister.
- Showing a book that has two dads cooking dinner for their child shows two parents caring for their son.
- Seeing a film with children talking about the many kinds of families that they are growing up in shows many ways that caring adults are raising children.

The resources in the Welcoming Schools Guide help students see love and concern for children as the common threads that run through caring families.

WE ARE TALKING ABOUT RESPECT.

In elementary school, the word "gay" is used widely as a put-down; often to mean that something is stupid. Students use the phrase "that's so gay" long before they know what the word "gay" means. Anti-LGBT or gender-related put-downs are among the most commonly heard slurs in school environments. When educators address the use of the word "gay," they are not introducing either the topic or the vocabulary.

When name-calling and put-downs are discussed it is important for educators to explicitly discuss the kinds of words that students are using. Words like gay or queer or sissy are words that hurt their classmates and friends. In these discussions on name-calling it is respect that is being discussed.

EXHIBIT 7.1 *continued*

SCHOOLS STRIVE TO INCREASE UNDERSTANDING AND CONNECTIONS ACROSS DIVERSITY OR DIFFERENCE.

Schools are places where many diverse people come together—many kinds of families, many races, many ethnicities and many faiths. Students and communities are best served when their members learn to get along with one another, understand one another and respect one another. Part of learning for students is to see and appreciate the diversity that exists in their classroom, their school, and the wider community. While there are differences, people also share much in common.

As our world and our interactions with people grow increasingly diverse, students benefit from developing the skills to live and work with many different kinds of people.

CHILDREN WITH SAME-SEX PARENTS ARE A RACIALLY, CULTURALLY AND GEOGRAPHICALLY DIVERSE GROUP.

Across America in suburban, rural and urban schools there are children with LGBT parents, grandparents or guardians.

- Households headed by same-sex couples are reported in virtually every US county according to the US Census.
- In rural states, such as Wyoming and Alaska, and in southern states households headed by same-sex couples are more likely to have children than same-sex households in other states.
- Hispanic and African-American same-sex couples are about twice as likely to be raising children as white non-Hispanic same-sex couples.

IT IS IMPORTANT FOR ALL CHILDREN TO BE A PART OF DISCUSSIONS OF FAMILIES, NAME-CALLING AND CURRENT EVENTS.

As our world becomes increasingly diverse, students will meet people—classmates, teammates, friends—with many kinds of families. Some will

EXHIBIT 7.1　*continued*

have parents, grandparents, guardians or other relatives who are gay, lesbian, bisexual or transgender. It is inevitable that discussions will and already do come up about what it means to be LGBT.

In today's environment the words "gay," "lesbian," "bisexual," or "transgender" come up in the context of current events. Students hear them in the news, in other media, and in many aspects of their lives. It can only be expected that when they come to school conversations and questions may arise in the classroom or in the hallways.

When students are not allowed to discuss LGBT-related topics, it heightens the mystery and potential divisiveness of the topic. All students benefit from discussions about family diversity, stopping put-downs and bullying, and exploring their curiosity and questions about current events.

In many states there are specific regulations for parental notification when the school curriculum addresses sexuality. However, when educators discuss family diversity, it is family—children's families—that is being discussed. In the lessons on name-calling, educators are discussing understanding and respect.

COMMUNICATION IS ESSENTIAL FOR BUILDING TRUST BETWEEN SCHOOL AND HOME.

It is important for parents/guardians to know what is going on in their child's classroom—whether it is about academics, such as the math unit they are covering, or about discussion of different kinds of families or hurtful LGBT-related or any other name-calling.

Some parents may feel more comfortable talking about their child's math lesson than talking about families with two moms or dads or about what "gay" or "lesbian" means. Parents may not know how to approach the topic with children. They may feel caught off-guard when a child asks about it. Knowing how these conversations happen at school can be helpful.

EXHIBIT 7.1   *continued*

Schools have successfully held evening forums that discuss families or that talk about how to handle hurtful teasing and bullying. Information for and communication with families is essential to building trust between school and home.

FAMILY RESPECT INCLUDES RESPECT FOR RELIGIOUS BELIEFS.

Public schools include people with many different religious beliefs. The role of schools is not to get everyone to agree but to foster a climate where there is respect for the diversity of beliefs and families within a community. Respect is built by acknowledging the diversity in the community, promoting opportunities for community dialogue and allowing the diversity of families to be visible within the school. Most people can agree that it is appropriate for schools to teach kindness and mutual respect for others' beliefs.

SCHOOLS ARE A PLACE FOR INFORMED AND OPEN DISCUSSIONS.

Information and discussion will not make anyone gay or straight. As students grow older, some will identify as gay, lesbian, bisexual or transgender. Most LGBT people grew up in households headed by heterosexual parents. On the other hand, knowing or learning about LGBT people might make someone less likely to insult or threaten someone he or she thinks is LGBT. Or, it might help someone not allow a friend to be ostracized for having an LGBT parent.

Reprinted with permission from *Welcoming Schools: An Inclusive Approach to Addressing Family Diversity, Gender Stereotyping, and Name-Calling in K–5 Learning Environments* (Washington DC: Human Rights Campaign Foundation, 2013).

EXHIBIT 8.1   Avon Community School Corporation 2012 strategic plan

According to Avon Schools Superintendent Maggie Hoerne-mann, the district's revised strategic plan served as a catalyst for broad-based cultural competence training, which in turn under-girded the school's progress in supporting LGBTQ students. Following is the text of the latest version of Avon's strategic plan.

AVON COMMUNITY SCHOOL CORPORATION
STRATEGIC PLAN—2012

1. Improve student achievement district-wide through individual student growth.
2. Establish a climate and culture that embraces all children, families, employees, and citizens of the Avon community.
3. Enhance communications at all levels to build stronger, richer, and more authentic relationships.
4. Support strategic initiatives through district-wide professional development.
5. Develop ongoing methods to maximize school district revenue and manage resources efficiently in support of this strategic plan.

APPENDIX B

Online Resources

EDUCATORS WHO WANT to create better schools for LGBTQ students work with varying levels of support from administration, school boards, and local communities. All educators, however, can tap into online resources to aid in their efforts. Following is a sampling of the web resources available in such areas as curriculum, student support services, and the growth and improvement of GSAs that can help educators move their schools to the next level, regardless of the point from which they are beginning.

PROGRAM DEVELOPMENT AND GSAS

Gay, Lesbian and Straight Education Network (GLSEN)

The GLSEN website (http://www.glsen.org) includes information about a wide range of issues that affect LGBTQ students in schools, including links to the executive summary and full report of the National School Climate Survey. Other resources include those for building and maintaining gay-straight alliances, educating teachers and school staff about the needs of LGBTQ youth, combating harassment and creating safer schools, and organizing in-school educational activities around commemorations such as No Name Calling Week and the National Day of Silence. The site also includes ordering information for resources such as safe space kits and state-by-state breakdowns of school climate data, as well as reports on issues affecting specific populations of LGBTQ youth, such as transgender students.

GSA Network

The California-based GSA Network (http://www.gsanetwork.org) provides information and assistance to educators and students around the country who want to start gay-straight alliances as well as those who wish to take existing GSAs the next level by making them sites for youth empowerment and leadership.

CURRICULUM

GroundSpark

GroundSpark (http://www.groundspark.com) produces films both for use with students and for professional development. These include the groundbreaking documentary *It's Elementary*, about addressing LGBTQ issues in elementary schools, and the follow-up *It's Still Elementary*, which follows some of the original participants into young adulthood. Additional films address the LGBTQ experience, bullying and harassment, and other issues relevant to students and educators. Through its "Respect for All" project, GroundSpark provides media resources, training, and support to educators, youth, and service providers.

Los Angeles Unified School District, LGBTQ Resources Page

The Los Angeles Unified School District maintains a website (http://notebook.lausd.net/portal/page?_pageid=33,1166406&_dad=ptl) with links to resources that educators from around the country can use in a variety of ways to improve schools for LGBTQ students. The resources come from multiple sources and include those for professional development; classroom lessons at the elementary, middle, and high school levels; and media such as PSAs and music videos related to LGBTQ issues.

Rainbow Book List, American Library Association

Created by the Gay, Lesbian, Bisexual, and Transgender Round Table of the American Library Association, the Rainbow Book List (http://glbtrt .ala.org/rainbowbooks/) is an annual annotated bibliography of books with LGBTQ-related content recommended for children up to age eighteen. Titles include both fiction and nonfiction as well as picture books. Lists are provided for every publication year going back to 2008.

Ready, Set, Respect!

Ready, Set, Respect! (http://www.glsen.org/readysetrespect) is a guide created by GLSEN in partnership with the National Association of Elementary School Principals and the National Association for the Education of Young Children to help elementary educators create safe and respectful learning environments. Lesson plans are aimed at helping teachers "seize teachable moments" about such issues as family diversity and gender roles, name calling, bullying, and cultural bias.

Safe Schools Coalition

Originally focused on the issues affecting schools in Washington State, the Safe Schools Coalition is now an organization that provides support to schools worldwide. Its website (http://www.safeschoolscoalition.org/RG-teachers_highschool.html) includes a variety of useful resources, including research reports, sample lesson plans, and resource lists for incorporating LGBTQ issues into K–12 curricula.

Unheard Voices: Stories of LGBT History

A collaboration of the Anti-Defamation League, GLSEN, and Story-Corps, Unheard Voices is an oral history and curriculum project intended to help educators incorporate LGBTQ topics into their curricula. The organization's website (http://www.adl.org/education/curriculum_connections/unheard-voices) includes links to audio interviews, which are supplemented by background and discussion questions as well as lesson plans for middle and high school classrooms.

Welcoming Schools

Welcoming Schools (http://www.welcomingschools.org) is an organization of the Human Rights Campaign Foundation dedicated to improving elementary schools and classrooms through education in three areas: family diversity, addressing gender stereotypes, and antibullying. Rather than a set curriculum, the *Welcoming Schools* guide is a resource book that includes lesson plans, handouts, and resource lists teachers can use in the classroom at various grade levels as well as materials for professional development, family education, and community building.

SUICIDE PREVENTION

Alex Project

Recognizing that text messaging is a primary mode of communication for today's youth, the Alex Project (http://www.alexproject.org) provides a twenty-four-hour text hotline to young people in crisis (text "LISTEN" to 741741) and "texting cards" that counselors and other educators can make available to students.

It Gets Better Project

Tens of thousands of videos have been created for the It Gets Better Project (http://www.itgetsbetter.org), whereby youth view and share messages of affirmation to counteract the negative effects of bullying and harassment in schools and society.

Trevor Project

The Trevor Project (http://www.trevorproject.org) is an organization dedicated to the prevention of LGBTQ youth suicide, including an online, confidential Q&A forum; Trevor Chat, a free, secure online messaging service staffed by trained volunteers; and a twenty-four-hour telephone hotline for youth, the Trevor Lifeline: 866-488-7386. Youth can also text "Trevor" to 1-202-304-1200.

OTHER STUDENT SUPPORTS

FIERCE

Fabulous Independent Educated Radicals for Community Empowerment, or FIERCE (http://www.fiercenyc.org), is a New York City–based organization dedicated to building leadership, self-expression, and the political organizing potential of LGBTQ youth of color both in New York and nationally. Among the resources on its website is the workshop curriculum for its LGBTQ Youth of Color Organizing Summit. The guide includes activities that can be used or modified to help young people in various settings understand different forms of oppression and how they intersect in society.

Gender Spectrum

Gender Spectrum (www.genderspectrum.org; info@genderspectrum.org) is an organization dedicated to helping create gender-sensitive and inclusive environments for children and adolescents. In addition to online resources and consultations and trainings with organizations that seek to be more gender inclusive, Gender Spectrum holds conferences and symposia to provide information and support to family members, to educators and other professionals, and to gender-expansive youth at the middle and high school levels. Its resources include an online "Gender Spectrum Lounge" for youth and families as well as a Spanish-language support group.

Point Foundation

The Point Foundation (http://www.pointfoundation.org) grants scholarships to LGBTQ-identifying youth for undergraduate and graduate study at colleges and universities. Each Point scholar is matched with an adult mentor who is a leader in the LGBTQ community. The foundation also helps connect LGBTQ youth with internship opportunities and holds an annual leadership conference for scholars and alumni.

WORKING WITH FAMILIES

PFLAG

Parents, Families, and Friends of Lesbians and Gays, or PFLAG (http://www.pflag.org), with chapters all over the United States, can help connect schools with speakers for professional development workshops and public events, provide resources for outreach to parents and families, and facilitate other school/family connections. PFLAG's "Get Support" section includes resources for families with LGBTQ members, such as a glossary of terms about LGBTQ issues, a "Family Story Center" where visitors can read and submit stories, and information about finding a local chapter.

TransYouth Family Allies

TransYouth Family Allies (http://www.imatyfa.org) forms partnerships with schools, service providers, and others to offer resources and support to transgender youth and their families. Services and resources include educational programs, a discussion group for parents, a speakers bureau, and advice about advocating for a transgender child's rights at school and in other contexts.

ADVOCACY

American Civil Liberties Union LGBT Youth and Schools Project

The ACLU's "LGBT Youth" page (http://www.aclu.org/lgbt-rights/lgbt-youth-schools) contains information about the legal rights associated with such topics as GSAs, antidiscrimination policies, harassment and bullying, proms and school dances, the "outing" of students or teachers, web filtering of LGBTQ-related content, free expression and censorship, and transgender issues. Phone assistance is available at 212-549-2673.

Lambda Legal

Lambda Legal (http://www.lambdalegal.org) is a nonprofit legal organization dedicated to defending the rights of LGBTQ individuals in a variety of circumstances, including the rights of youth in schools and other settings. Lambda Legal's help desk responds to inquiries by individuals who believe they may have experienced discrimination on the basis of sexual orientation, gender identity and expression, or HIV status: 1-866-542-8336.

NOTES

INTRODUCTION

1. Roger Simon, "Empowerment as a Pedagogy of Possibility," *Language Arts* 64, no. 4 (April 1987): 370–382.

2. Many writers and advocates also include the letter *I* to refer to intersex individuals—people born with sexual characteristics that would be considered both male and female in the binary paradigm. Intersex rights advocates have called for change in the medical community to end practices aimed at "normalizing" children at birth to conform to one sex or another. Because none of the school programs I profile here address this issue discretely, I do not include this letter in the abbreviation.

3. This organization is now known as the Massachusetts Commission on LGBTQ Youth.

4. Michael Sadowski, "Creating Safer Schools: The Beginning of Gay and Lesbian Student Rights in Massachusetts" (unpublished paper, Governor's Commission on Gay and Lesbian Youth, 2002).

5. For a description of the Safe Schools Coalition and links to its research publications, see safeschoolscoalition.org.

6. For a discussion of the controversies surrounding Harvey Milk High School in the early 2000s, see John Colapinto, "The Harvey Milk School Has No Right to Exist. Discuss," *New York* magazine, February 7, 2005, nymag.com/nymetro/news/features/10970/index5.html.

7. www.hmi.org/hmhs

8. Dean Praetorius, "Jamey Rodemeyer, 14-Year-Old Boy, Commits Suicide After Gay Bullying, Parents Carry on Message." *Huffington Post*, September 20, 2011, http://www.huffingtonpost.com/2011/09/20/jamey-rodemeyer-suicide-gay-bullying_n_972023.html

9. See www.iowasafeschools.org/index.php/about-iowa-safe-schools.

10. Gay, Lesbian and Straight Education Network, "Enumeration" (policy statement), http://www.glsen.org/sites/default/files/Enumeration_0.pdf.

11. Joseph G. Kosciw, Emily A. Greytak, Neal A. Palmer, and Maddy J. Boesen, *The 2013 National School Climate Survey: The Experiences of Lesbian, Gay, Bisexual and Transgender Youth in Our Nation's Schools* (New York: GLSEN, 2014), www.glsen.org/article/2013-national-school-climate-survey.

12. Nan Stein, "Bullying or Sexual Harassment? The Missing Discourse of Rights in an Era of Zero Tolerance," *Arizona Law Review* 45 (2003): 783–799.

13. www.glsen.org/safespace

14. http://notebook.lausd.net/portal/
    page?_pageid=33,1159973&_dad=ptl&_schema=PTL_EP

15. Kosciw et al., *The 2013 National School Climate Survey.*

16. Ibid.

17. Stephen T. Russell et al., "Youth Empowerment and High School Gay-Straight Alliances." *Journal of Youth and Adolescence* 38, no. 7 (2009): 891–903.

18. Massachusetts was one of the first states to track youth risk behaviors by sexual orientation and arguably has the most comprehensive data on the risk behaviors of LGBTQ adolescents and how patterns have changed and/or remained consistent over the last two decades. See "Massachusetts High School Students and Sexual Orientation: Results of the 2013 Youth Risk Behavior Survey," http://www.mass.gov/cgly/YRBS13_FactsheetUpdated.pdf.

19. www.gallup.com/poll/1651/gay-lesbian-rights.aspx

20. Kosciw et al., *The 2013 National School Climate Survey.*

21. Ibid.

22. Ibid.

CHAPTER 1

1. Joseph G. Kosciw, Emily A. Greytak, Neal A. Palmer, and Maddy J. Boesen, *The 2013 National School Climate Survey: The Experiences of Lesbian, Gay, Bisexual and Transgender Youth in Our Nation's Schools* (New York: GLSEN, 2014), www.glsen.org/article/2013-national-school-climate-survey.

2. Arthur Lipkin, *Understanding Homosexuality: Changing Schools* (Boulder, CO: Westview Press, 1999), 327–328.

3. See, for example, John P. Anders, *Willa Cather's Sexual Aesthetics and the Male Homosexual Literary Tradition* (Lincoln: University of Nebraska Press, 1999).

4. Vito Russo et al., *The Celluloid Closet*, directed by Rob Epstein and Jeffrey Friedman (Los Angeles: Sony Pictures Classics, 1996).

5. For a summary of stage theories of lesbian and gay identity development, see Lipkin, *Understanding Homosexuality*, 99–116.

6. Amy Ellis Nutt, *Becoming Nicole: The Transformation of an American Family* (New York: Random House, 2015).

7. Kimberle Crenshaw, "Mapping the Margins: Intersectionality, Identity Politics, and Violence Against Women of Color," *Stanford Law Review* 43, no. 6 (1991): 1241–1299.

8. Debra Scherban, "ARHS Teacher Barber-Just One of Four Nationally Honored by Williams College," *Daily Hampshire Gazette*, July 20, 2014, http://www.gazettenet.com/home/12429920-95/arhs-teacher-barber-just-one-of-four-nationally-honored-by-williams-college.

9. Personal correspondence with the author, August 26, 2015.

10. Personal correspondence with the author, August 28, 2015.

11. Michelle Alexander, *The New Jim Crow: Mass Incarceration in the Age of Colorblindness* (New York: New Press, 2010).

12. Margot Stern Strom, *Facing History and Ourselves: Holocaust and Human Behavior* (Brookline, MA: Facing History and Ourselves, 1994).

13. For a more detailed explanation of the term *guevedoche*, which refers to children raised as female who develop male sex characteristics at puberty, see Gilbert Herdt (ed.), *Third Sex, Third Gender: Beyond Sexual Dimorphism in History* (New York: Zone Books, 1993).

14. Cornell University maintains a useful website on the history of the LGBTQ rights movement based on the records of the Human Rights Campaign, which includes a discussion of the homophile movement of the 1950s and 1960s: rmc.library.cornell.edu/HRC/exhibition/stage/stage_3.html

15. The LAUSD resolution on LGBT inclusion is available online at notebook.lausd.net. (Enter "LGBT resolution" in search field.)

16. See resource list on pp. 187–193.

17. Massachusetts Governor's Commission on Gay and Lesbian Youth (MCGLY), "Recommendations of the Governor's Commission on Gay and Lesbian Youth Based on Testimony Received at the Commission's 10th Anniversary Forums" (Boston: MCGLY, 2004).

18. Elizabeth J. Meyer, *Gender and Sexual Diversity in Schools: An Introduction* (New York: Springer, 2010), 70–76.

19. Cris Mayo, *LGBTQ Youth and Education: Policies and Practices* (New York: Teachers College Press, 2014), 78.

20. According to the Gay, Lesbian and Straight Education Network, the following states have "no promo homo" laws on their books: Alabama, Arizona, Louisiana, Mississippi, Oklahoma, South Carolina, Texas, and Utah. See www.glsen.org/learn/policy/issues/nopromohomo.

CHAPTER 2

1. nationalseedproject.org
2. Winnie Hu, "At a Long Island Middle School, A Course in What Unites and Divides," *New York Times*, October 22, 2010, www.nytimes.com/2010/10/23/nyregion/23metjournal.html.
3. Michael Sadowski, *In a Queer Voice: Journeys of Resilience from Adolescence to Adulthood* (Philadelphia: Temple University Press, 2013).
4. Joseph G. Kosciw, Emily A. Greytak, Neal A. Palmer, and Maddy J. Boesen, *The 2013 National School Climate Survey: The Experiences of Lesbian, Gay, Bisexual and Transgender Youth in Our Nation's Schools* (New York: GLSEN, 2014), www.glsen.org/article/2013-national-school-climate-survey.
5. Peter C. Scales and Nancy Leffert, *Developmental Assets: A Synthesis of the Scientific Research on Adolescent Development*, 2nd ed. (Minneapolis: Search Institute, 2004), 36–38.
6. Kosciw et al., *The 2013 National School Climate Survey*.
7. Kelly S. Kennedy, "Accessing Community Resources: Providing Support for All," in *Creating Safe and Supportive Learning Environments: A Guide for Working with Lesbian, Gay, Bisexual, Transgender, and Questioning Youth and Families*, eds. Emily S. Fisher and Karen Komosa-Hawkins (New York: Routledge, 2013), 243–255.
8. Asaf Orr and Karen Komosa-Hawkins. "Law, Policy, and Ethics: What School Professionals Need to Know." In Fisher and Komosa-Hawkins, *Creating Safe and Supportive Learning Environments*, 116.

CHAPTER 3

1. ag.org/top/beliefs/relations_11_homosexual.cfm
2. From acceptance speech delivered at GLSEN Respect Awards, New York, June 1, 2015.
3. Zach Wahls, *My Two Moms: Lessons of Love, Strength, and What Makes a Family* (New York: Gotham, 2012).

4. KSPR News (ABC), April 20, 2015. Clip available at www.kspr.com.

5. According to the Gay, Lesbian and Straight Education Network, the following states have "no promo homo" laws on their books: Alabama, Arizona, Louisiana, Mississippi, Oklahoma, South Carolina, Texas, and Utah. See www.glsen.org/learn/policy/issues/nopromohomo.

6. Stephanie Mencimer, "Mormon Church Abandons Its Crusade Against Gay Marriage," *Mother Jones*, April 12, 2013, http://www.motherjones .com/politics/2013/04/prop-8-mormons-gay-marriage-shift.

7. The Alex Project's mission is to help prevent youth suicide by making text messaging "hotline" resources available to teens in crisis. See www .alexproject.org.

8. See the Park City GSA's online portfolio at https://pchgsa.allyou.net.

9. Albert B. Bandura, *Self-Efficacy: The Exercise of Control* (New York: W. H. Freeman, 1997).

10. See, for example, Pedro Noguera, "Joaquin's Dilemma: Understanding the Link Between Racial Identity and School-Related Behaviors," in *Adolescents at School: Perspectives on Youth, Identity, and Education*, 2nd ed., ed. Michael Sadowski (Cambridge, MA: Harvard Education Press, 2008), 23–34.

11. Stephen T. Russell et al., "Youth Empowerment and High School Gay-Straight Alliances," *Journal of Youth and Adolescence* 38, no. 7 (2009): 891–903.

12. For information about the Allie the Ally Project, see allietheally .tumblr.com.

13. Sadowski, *In a Queer Voice*.

14. From acceptance speeches delivered at GLSEN Respect Awards, New York, June 1, 2015.

CHAPTER 4

1. Nancy L. Deutsch, *Pride in the Projects: Teens Building Identities in Urban Contexts* (New York: New York University Press, 2008), 10.

2. Ibid.

3. Joe Wilson and Dean Hamer, "From Film Campaign to National Award," *Huffington Post*, December 10, 2011, http://outinthesilence.blogspot .com/2011_12_01_archive.html.

4. Personal correspondence with the author, August 21, 2015.

5. Janet Mock, *Redefining Realness: My Path to Womanhood, Identity, Love and So Much More* (New York: Atria Books, 2014).

6. Joseph G. Kosciw, Emily A. Greytak, Neal A. Palmer, and Maddy J. Boesen, *The 2013 National School Climate Survey: The Experiences of Lesbian, Gay, Bisexual and Transgender Youth in Our Nation's Schools* (New York: GLSEN, 2014), www.glsen.org/article/2013-national-school-climate-survey.

7. Ibid.

8. Asaf Orr and Karen Komosa-Hawkins, "Law, Policy, and Ethics: What School Professionals Need to Know," in *Creating Safe and Supportive Learning Environments: A Guide for Working with Lesbian, Gay, Bisexual, Transgender, and Questioning Youth and Families*, eds. Emily S. Fisher and Karen Komosa-Hawkins (New York: Routledge, 2013), 110.

9. For a national profile of nondiscrimination policies affecting LGBTQ individuals, see the Human Rights Campaign web page, www.hrc.org/resources/entry/workplace-discrimination-policies-laws-and-legislation.

10. Kimberle Crenshaw, "Mapping the Margins: Intersectionality, Identity Politics, and Violence Against Women of Color," *Stanford Law Review* 43, no. 6 (1991): 1241–1299.

11. Jean E. Rhodes, *Stand by Me: The Risks and Rewards of Mentoring Today's Youth* (Cambridge, MA: Harvard University Press, 2002).

12. Chapters of Parents, Families, and Friends of Lesbians and Gays (PFLAG) exist all over the country and are a resource for consultation, speakers, and other help in working with families of LGBTQ youth: www.pflag.org.

13. See, for example, Jill McLean Taylor, Carmen N. Veloria, and Martina C. Verba, "Latina Girls: 'We're Like Sisters—Most Times!'" in *Urban Girls Revisited: Building Strengths*, eds. Bonnie J. Ross Leadbeater and Niobe Way (New York: New York University Press, 2007), 157–174.

14. Jennifer Pastor et al., "Makin' Homes: An Urban Girl Thing," in *Urban Girls Revisited: Building Strengths*, eds. Bonnie J. Ross Leadbeater and Niobe Way (New York: New York University Press, 2007), 75–96.

CHAPTER 5

1. Joseph G. Kosciw, Emily A. Greytak, Neal A. Palmer, and Maddy J. Boesen, *The 2013 National School Climate Survey: The Experiences of Lesbian, Gay, Bisexual and Transgender Youth in Our Nation's Schools* (New York: GLSEN, 2014), www.glsen.org/article/2013-national-school-climate-survey.

2. Ibid.

3. Kathleen E. Rands, "Considering Transgender People in Education: A Gender-Complex Approach," *Journal of Teacher Education* 60, no. 4 (2009): 419–431.

4. GLSEN also provides a model school district policy on the issues affecting transgender students on its website: www.glsen.org/article/transgender-model-district-policy.

5. See, for example, Rebecca Hagelin, "California Strips Privacy from Kids: The Coed Bathroom Law" at drjamesdobson.org/specials/ca-coed-bathroom-law.

6. Holly Yan, "California Law Lets Transgender Students Pick Bathrooms, Teams to Join," August 13, 2013, CNN.com, www.cnn.com/2013/08/13/US/california-transgender-school-law.

7. Autumn Sandeen, "Interview with LAUSD's Judy Chiasson About AB1266," *TransAdvocate*, January 18, 2014, http://www.transadvocate.com/interview-with-lausds-judy-chiasson-about-ab1266_n_11351.htm.

8. Jacqueline Woodson, *From the Notebooks of Melanin Sun* (New York: Scholastic, 1995).

9. Emily A. Greytak and Joseph G. Kosciw, "Responsive Classroom Curriculum for Lesbian, Gay, Bisexual, Transgender, and Questioning Students," in *Creating Safe and Supportive Learning Environments: A Guide for Working with Lesbian, Gay, Bisexual, Transgender, and Questioning Youth and Families*, eds. Emily S. Fisher and Karen Komosa-Hawkins (New York: Routledge, 2013), 159.

10. Sassafras Lowrey, ed., *Kicked Out* (Ypsilanti, MI: Homofactus Press, 2010).

11. Genny Beemyn, "The Children Should Lead Us: Diane Ehrensaft's Gender Born, Gender Made: Raising Healthy Gender Nonconforming Children," *Journal of LGBT Youth*, no. 10 (2013): 159–162.

CHAPTER 6

1. Norman Garmezy, "Children in Poverty: Resilience Despite Risk," *Psychiatry* 56, no. 1 (1993): 127–136; Michael Rutter, "Psychosocial Resilience and Protective Mechanisms," *Journal of Orthopsychiatry* 57, no. 3 (1987): 316–331.

2. Michael Sadowski, *Portraits of Promise: Voices of Successful Immigrant Students* (Cambridge, MA: Harvard Education Press, 2013); Michael

Sadowski, *In a Queer Voice: Journeys of Resilience from Adolescence to Adulthood* (Philadelphia: Temple University Press, 2013); Carola Suarez-Orozco, Marcelo M. Suarez-Orozco, and Irina Todorova, *Learning a New Land: Immigrant Students in American Society* (Cambridge, MA: Belknap Press of Harvard University Press, 2008).

3. Joseph G. Kosciw, Emily A. Greytak, Neal A. Palmer, and Maddy J. Boesen, *The 2013 National School Climate Survey: The Experiences of Lesbian, Gay, Bisexual and Transgender Youth in Our Nation's Schools* (New York: GLSEN, 2014), www.glsen.org/article/2013-national-school-climate-survey.

4. Sadowski, *In a Queer Voice*, 144.

5. Ibid.

6. Personal correspondence with the author, August 26, 2014.

7. Mary Kay Schoen, "Gay and Lesbian School Counselors: Making a Difference," *School Counselor*, May–June 2011, https://www.schoolcounselor .org/magazine/blogs/may-june-2011/ gay-and-lesbian-school-counselors-making-a-differ.

8. Malinda Lo, *Ash* (Boston: Little Brown, 2010); David Levithan, *Boy Meets Boy* (New York: Knopf, 2005).

9. Emily Style, "Curriculum as Window and Mirror," *Social Science Record*, Fall 1996, www.wcwonline.org/SEED/seed-curriculum-as-window-a-mirror.

10. LGBTQIA generally stands for lesbian, gay, bisexual, transgender, queer, questioning, intersex, and asexual.

11. Marion Dane Bauer, *Am I Blue? Coming Out from the Silence* (New York: Harper, 1995).

12. Massachusetts Department of Elementary and Secondary Education, "Massachusetts High School Students and Sexual Orientation: Results of the 2013 Youth Risk Behavior Survey" (Malden, MA: Massachusetts Department of Education, 2013), http://www.mass.gov/cgly/YRBS13_ FactsheetUpdated.pdf.

13. Sadowski, *In a Queer Voice*.

14. Joan F. Kaywell, *Dear Author: Letters of Hope* (New York: Philomel Books, 2007).

15. Sadowski, *In a Queer Voice*.

16. Phone interview with the author, August 2015.

17. Hazel Markus and Paula Nurius, "Possible Selves," *American Psychologist* 41, no. 9 (September 1986): 954–69.

18. Sadowski, *In a Queer Voice*.

19. Maria E. Gonzalez, "School Counselor Advocacy with LGBT Students: A Qualitative Study of High School Counselor Experiences (unpublished dissertation, University of Massachusetts–Amherst, 2014), 165.

CHAPTER 7

1. Cris Mayo, *LGBTQ Youth and Education: Policies and Practices* (New York: Teachers College Press, 2014), 32–33.
2. Minnesota Family Council, "*Star Tribune* Spin Ignores Legitimate Concerns Regarding 'Welcoming Schools,'" May 18, 2008, http://mnfamilycouncil .blogspot.com/2008/05/star-tribune-spin-ignores-legitimate.html.
3. Katherine Pillsbury et al., *The Welcoming Schools Guide: An Inclusive Approach to Addressing Family Diversity, Gender Stereotyping and Name-Calling in K–5 Learning Environments* (Washington DC: Human Rights Campaign Foundation, 2013), B-8.
4. Pillsbury et al., *The Welcoming Schools Guide*, B-25–B-27.
5. Ibid.
6. Kathryn Otoshi, *One* (Mill Valley, CA: KO Kids Books, 2008).
7. Centers for Disease Control and Prevention, "Suicide: Facts at a Glance" (Washington DC: CDC, 2015), http://www.cdc.gov/violenceprevention/ pdf/suicide-datasheet-a.pdf.
8. The Gay, Lesbian and Straight Education Network also publishes a guide to approaching LGBT issues with elementary school students called "Ready, Set, Respect," at http://www.glsen.org/readysetrespect.
9. Richard Sagor, *Guiding School Improvement with Action Research* (Washington DC: Association for Supervision and Curriculum Development, 2000).
10. Personal correspondence with the author, October 13, 2014.
11. Marcus Ewart, *10,000 Dresses* (New York: Triangle Square Press, 2008); Justin Richardson and Peter Parnell, *And Tango Makes Three* (New York: Simon & Schuster, 2005); Linda De Haan and Stern Nijland, *King and King* (Berkeley, CA: Tricycle Press, 2003); Justin Richardson and Peter Parnell, *Christian, the Hugging Lion* (New York: Simon & Schuster, 2010); Harvey Fierstein, *The Sissy Duckling* (New York: Simon & Schuster, 2002); Ian Falconer, *Olivia* (New York: Atheneum Books, 2000).
12. Alexandria Hollett, "Unpacking Gender and Identity Stereotypes in a Second Grade Classroom" (presentation to Action Research Leadership Institute, Chicago, May 2012).

13. Mayo, *LGBTQ Youth and Education*, 33.
14. Elizabeth J. Meyer, *Gender and Sexual Diversity in Schools: An Introduction* (New York: Springer, 2010, 64–65).
15. Meyer, *Gender and Sexual Diversity in Schools*, 65–66.
16. Pillsbury et al. *The Welcoming Schools Guide*, B-3–B-4.
17. Ibid.
18. Teresa Bouley, as cited in Meyer, *Gender and Sexual Diversity in Schools*, 80.

CHAPTER 8

1. http://www.avon-schools.org/Page/7526.
2. Gary Howard, *We Can't Teach What We Don't Know: White Teachers, Multiracial Schools* (New York: Teachers College Press, 1999).

AFTERWORD

1. Massachusetts Department of Elementary and Secondary Education, "Massachusetts High School Students and Sexual Orientation: Results of the 2013 Youth Risk Behavior Survey" (Malden, MA: Massachusetts Department of Education, 2013), http://www.mass.gov/cgly/YRBS13_FactsheetUpdated.pdf.
2. Joseph G. Kosciw, Emily A. Greytak, Neal A. Palmer, and Maddy J. Boesen, *The 2013 National School Climate Survey: The Experiences of Lesbian, Gay, Bisexual and Transgender Youth in Our Nation's Schools* (New York: GLSEN, 2014), www.glsen.org/article/2013-national-school-climate-survey.

ACKNOWLEDGMENTS

ALTHOUGH THE MAIN premise of this book is that "safe" is not enough, none of the ideas profiled here would have been possible without the groundbreaking work of the dedicated individuals who built the "safe schools" movement in the 1980s and 1990s. These people risked their careers and sometimes even their safety because they knew LGBTQ youth were at risk in their schools, and they advocated for change at a time when they had few political allies. They often faced hostile reception from school administrators, community members, parents, and advocates for the "religious right." It would be impossible to list their names without a glaring omission, but those whose work was particularly influential in my own development as an LGBTQ youth advocate include Bernie Gardella, Kathleen Henry, Kevin Jennings, Michael Kozuch, David LaFontaine, Arthur Lipkin, Vincent McCarthy, Bob Parlin, Carlene Pavlos, Jeff Perrotti, Beth Reis, James Sears, Grace Sterling Stowell, Virginia Uribe, and Kim Westheimer. These people and others like them are the heroes not only of the students with whom they have worked directly but also of those who continue to benefit from the evolution of the movement beyond "safe" to this day.

The Gay, Lesbian and Straight Education Network continues to save lives with the critical work it does on many fronts to improve school climates for LGBTQ students. I'm especially grateful to GLSEN research director Emily Greytak and former education director Robert McGarry for the advice and guidance they provided in the early stages of this project.

Obviously, this book would not be possible without the teachers, administrators, counselors, staff members, and especially students who so generously gave of their time and insights to be interviewed. They are the modern-day heroes of this story, as they make a difference every day they walk into their school buildings. In addition to those mentioned throughout the chapters, other teachers who contributed valuable insights as this book was developing include Patricia Carlin, Nicholas Ferroni, Lisa Koenecke, and my husband, teacher and GSA advisor Robb Fessler. In addition to proofreading and entering corrections when my fingers couldn't handle one more keystroke, Robb served as a constant source of inspiration through his dedication both to me and to his students. He kept telling me this was a book teachers and kids needed, and that drove me to keep pushing.

In that vein, I also owe a huge debt of gratitude to Harvard Education Publishing Group Executive Director Doug Clayton, who has always believed in and championed my work, and to the team at Harvard Education Press, including Laura Clos, Laura Cutone Godwin, Rachel Monaghan, Sumita Mukherji, and especially Editor-in-Chief Caroline Chauncey. Without Caroline's guidance, this wouldn't be half the book it is today. When I couldn't see the forest for the trees, Caroline helped me see where the manuscript needed to go, gave me the push I needed to meet deadlines (or at least approximate them), and cheered me on with her unfailing enthusiasm. Every author should be so lucky to have an editor like Caroline on their side.

ABOUT THE AUTHOR

Michael Sadowski teaches about youth development and education at Bard College and is director of the Bard Early College–Hudson Initiative, a program to offer Bard courses to high school students in New York's Hudson Valley. He is the author of *In a Queer Voice: Journeys of Resilience from Adolescence to Adulthood* (Temple University Press, 2013) and *Portraits of Promise: Voices of Successful Immigrant Students* (Harvard Education Press, 2013). He also is the editor of the Harvard Education Press book series on youth development and education; *Adolescents at School: Perspectives on Youth, Identity, and Education*, now in its second edition with Harvard Education Press; and *Teaching Immigrant and Second-Language Students: Strategies for Success* (Harvard Education Press, 2004). He has written numerous articles and book chapters for publications such as *Educational Leadership*, *Issues in Teacher Education*, and the *Encyclopedia of the Life Course and Human Development*, and he has contributed op-ed pieces to the LGBTQ news magazine the *Advocate*. In addition, Michael was editor of the *Harvard Education Letter*, for which he won the National Press Club Award for analytical newsletter journalism; served as a faculty member at the Harvard Graduate School of Education; was vice-chair of the Massachusetts Governor's Commission on Gay and Lesbian Youth; and taught high school and middle school English and theatre at public schools in New York and Massachusetts.

INDEX